Restorative Justice

Restorative Justice

Healing the Effects of Crime

Jim Consedine

PLOUGHSHARES PUBLICATIONS

In honour of

JEAN STEWART

prophet, activist, Christian woman,
founder and president of the
Movement for Alternatives to Prison

and

In memory of my niece

SUZANNE ELIZABETH CONSEDINE

a bright, beautiful, compassionate, loving, wise and generous spirit who
brought an enormous amount of laughter, joy and tears to us all,
accidentally killed at Anakiwa,
3 August 1993

ISBN 0-473-02992-8
Copyright © 1995 Jim Consedine

Published by Ploughshares Publications, PO Box 173, Lyttelton, New Zealand.
Ploughshares Publications is a branch of Te Wairua Maranga Trust, Otautahi/Christchurch, New Zealand.

Production and design by Orca Publishing Services, Christchurch, New Zealand. Printed in Australia.

Contents

Acknowledgments

Many people have shared ideas and energy to help bring this book to fruition. The most vital role has been filled by Sue McNabb, at whose word processor I have sat for hundreds of hours mulling over the text, getting the sequence muddled and jamming the printer. Sue has not only unveiled the intricacies of computers to me, but unravelled the mess I've occasionally created, and offered critical comment on structure. Her commitment to the book has been unwavering, her kindness, generosity and support integral to its publication. I thank her sincerely.

Special thanks too must go to Cynthia Brooks for her editing. Her generous response to my invitation to edit reflects her kind and expansive spirit. Needless to say, any brickbats regarding the quality of the final copy should come my way, not hers – her job was simply to supply the spit and polish to my rather garrulous original text.

A special word of thanks also to Judge Michael Brown of Nga Puhi and Ngati Kahu, who humbled me with the content of his foreword. If ever history bestows an honour on the single most influential figure in the modern-day development of restorative justice in Aotearoa, it should go to Mick Brown. His pioneering work on youth justice set the scene for later developments both in the formulation of the Children, Young Persons and Their Families Act, and in the field of adult restorative processes.

Thanks too to various people for insights into differing chapters. Thanks to Waha Stirling of Ngai Tahu and Ngati Porou, who said this book 'had to be written', and to Judge Fred McElrea, who shares a passion for restorative justice and has the mind and courage to match his ideas. Thanks also to that prophetic figure Moana Jackson of Ngati Porou and Ngati Kohungunu for his research, encouragement and insights, which helped me understand a different but equally important vision of criminal justice for Aotearoa.

I am exremely grateful to Malama Meleisea for his guidance with the Samoan chapter, to Peter Norden S.J., of Melbourne, and Dr Bob Bellear, of Sydney, for hospitality offered and encouragement given while I researched the Australian and Aboriginal chapters, and to Howard Zehr, whose inspired writings and vision first set me alight with the possibilities for restorative justice in this country.

My thanks also go to Alan Gower, who cured a dreadful virus in the computer that looked like streptococci. Thanks too to Lesley Knight, who designed the cover; Marge Pollock for the logo; Martin Woodhall for the photo; and Lesley and Peter Croucher for their ideas. Thanks also to Quentin Wilson and Rachel Scott of Orca Publishing Services for advice and encouragement.

Finally, thanks must go to my basic family groupings: my own immediate family, with whom I share a vision of justice implanted within us by our parents; the Christchurch Prison Chaplains team, who have nourished me spiritually and sustained me week in week out for many years; the members of St Joseph the Worker Parish in Lyttelton and Diamond Harbour, with whom it is a privilege to live and worship; and the extended Catholic Worker community, who offer daily friendship and support in the work of building a more just and caring society.

We are all interconnected, woven together by the grace of God and the love we share. This book is a fruit of that process in which my role, though pivotal, owes much to countless others.

Foreword

I have been involved as a practitioner in the criminal justice field for about 30 years, the last 15 of which have been as a District Court judge. For a great deal of that time I have been invaded by reservations as to our present punitive practices, which in turn have led me from time to time to question my own participation in such a system. The rationalisation that perhaps it can be better changed from within that has subdued and dulled that dilemma but never laid it to rest.

For almost a decade, between 1980 and the end of 1989, I was a District Court judge in West Auckland, where I had the opportunity of observing and working with such enlightened people as Dr Peter Sharples and his team at Hoani Waititi Marae. Of particular interest was their work with Maori committees involving Maori youth who had offended. By taking matters out of the courtroom and using other venues such as marae or even school grounds, a much more egalitarian environment, I began to sense that there may be alternative ways of handling these matters.

By changing the emphasis from a punitive condemnatory stance to one where the group sought to repair the emotional and material damage of crime, I glimpsed the potential for a wider applicability of such a process and the capacity for far more creative resolution of problems.

With the advent of the Children, Young Persons and Their Families Act in 1989, particularly with the provisions for family group conferences, my enthusiasm blossomed. The undeniable success of that process with its exciting and limitless potential, particularly for victim involvement and input, has been a wonderful experience. The robustness of the exercise and the enthusiastic involvement of the police Youth Aid Section made this a most satisfying and encouraging area within which to work.

As a result various questions have presented themselves. Could we place this technique in some historical context? Is this a procedure amenable only to the Maori mind? Is this process limited only to the New Zealand situation? Does it work for other young offenders?

Subsequent interest from most of the Australian states, Britain, the United States, Sweden and South Africa has provided stimulating exchanges. In particular, the approval and support from such distinguished international scholars as Dr John Braithwaite and Professor D. L. Nathanson, as well as constructive discussion from such New Zealand scholars as Dr Gabrielle Maxwell and Dr Allison Morris, have provided an exciting stimulus to this work.

In New Zealand the research work done by my brother judge F. W. M. McElrea after study leave at Cambridge University has added a further intellectual rigidity to the concept of a restorative model. Similarly, a recent visit by Dr Howard Zehr enabled us to compare notes on work being done independently in the United States.

Now we have this significant contribution from Father Jim Consedine. In his first section on retributive justice he articulates those flaws that I and others had sensed in our present system and, in taking a comparative view from other jurisdictions, exposes the pointlessness and waste, both in fiscal terms and, more importantly, in terms of human destruction and degradation, serving only to compound the problem rather than find the solution.

This is aptly captured in Chapter 11, where he says:

> The millions of dollars we waste on building new prisons and maintaining our old ones is, generally speaking, money wasted. In no other area of public tax funds expenditure do public monies get less scrutiny in terms of positive effectiveness than in the area of penal policy.

This book is not just another diatribe against penal policy. Rather I see it as a powerful polemic, carefully sourced and widely researched, which offers a closely argued possible alternative solution.

By drawing together the universality of the restorative process with its biblical roots and even wider derivation with other cultures, the book and its message could be a blueprint for a vision that is so badly needed in contemporary Western society.

Jim Consedine's unique experience and contact with prisoners over a long period must lend to this volume a special credibility.

Apart from those marvellous insights, after so long an exposure to the raw side of humanity, it is the essential essence of Christian humanity pervading the book that makes the reader so conscious of the potential of the human spirit.

Michael J. A. Brown
Principal Youth Court Judge
Auckland, New Zealand
6 October 1994

Introduction

The families of two South Auckland boys killed by a car welcomed the accused driver yesterday with open arms and forgiveness. The young man, who gave himself up to the police yesterday morning, apologised to the families and was ceremonially reunited with the Tongan and Samoan communities at a special church service last night.

The 20-year-old Samoan visited the Tongan families after his court appearance yesterday to apologise for the deaths of the two children in Mangere last Tuesday. The Tongan and Samoan communities of Mangere later gathered at the Tongan Methodist Church in a service of reconciliation. The young man sat at the feast table flanked by the mothers of the dead boys.

NZPA, 21 December 1993

One of the most lasting television images of 1993 had to be that of the families of two South Auckland boys killed by a car welcoming, with open arms and forgiveness, the accused driver and his family.

What a contrast to the normal reaction we have come to expect via the media to such highly charged deaths of young children. Time and again, admittedly often in more dramatic circumstances, an enraged family (and sometimes it seems a whole township) has gathered outside the home of the accused calling for vengeance, and on several occasions forcing the family to flee for their own safety. Here all the pent-up violence, frustration and fear of a community can be unleashed in an orgy of name-calling, rock-throwing and threats of physical violence to the families of the accused.

How different the scene in Mangere was! Here several important values came into play to create a constructive mechanism to deal with the grief the community was experiencing. Two major threads interwove to build reconciliation and forgiveness. Firstly, both Tongan and Samoan communities have a tradition of restorative justice when it comes to offending in the community. This means that the wellbeing of the community and its restoration to peace and harmony are the primary values sought in the justice process.

So restoring the young man to his family and restoring the good bonds between the two communities were the primary objects. The offer of a sincere apology and its acceptance through forgiveness and mercy form the natural flow-on from such a tradition. Sanction forms a less important part of the proceedings.

Secondly, the deeply held Christian beliefs of both communities meant that they recognised each other as belonging to the one family of God that even national boundaries and culpable action should not place at risk. Hence the faith of the families and the communities generally meant that reconciliation and healing could be achieved even before the processes of the law got fully under way.

In Christian terms, the Word did become flesh in South Auckland in this Christmas-week tragedy. In seeking true justice based on values of honesty, forgiveness and mercy leading to reconciliation and healing, the Tongan and Samoan communities became midwives to the birth of Christ in their midst. No amount of tinsel – not even Santa – could deny the truth of that birth.

And who will ever forget the smile of Nelson Mandela and the joyous dance of Archbishop Desmond Tutu as they cast their first ever vote in a general election in South Africa? Even more striking was the message they jointly shared with the watching world. After years of enslavement, imprisonment, violence, poverty, oppression, death and racism of the worst kind, their joint message was not one of vengeance, punishment and 'just desserts' but of restoration, healing, mercy and forgiveness. Here was restorative justice in practice on a global scale. They gave spiritual and moral direction to the whole world.

The alternative response happens in mainstream society every day. We rely too often on the law, by itself a soulless set of rules, to attempt to see justice achieved. In effect, there are no mechanisms in mainstream society for reconciliation to be achieved from such a tragedy. Within the confines of the social structures of mainstream law, apology and sorrow cannot meet mercy, forgiveness and reconciliation. Instead the victims and their families are shut out of the processes from day one, and the offender awaits his or her just desserts, often in isolation, always in fear and trepidation. This usually happens in a prison cell, cut off from grieving families on both sides of the tragedy.

The consequence of this situation is an almost total lack of healing for the offender and the victim, resulting in a residue of deep bitterness and anger that can last for years.

Would that our wider society could learn from the wisdom and traditions of Polynesian New Zealanders. Maori have a tradition of restorative justice, still in effect in many rural areas, whereby the restoration of all concerned – the victims, the offenders, the whanau, the iwi – is the principal objective.

Such a process allows a human face to be put on offending, and allows healing to occur in place of bitterness, mercy to be effected in place of retribution, and constructive sanctions to be put in place instead of useless ones such as imprisonment.

Another short illustration. In September 1994, a young Maori man in Northland was shot three times by a policeman when he tried to run away and avoid a breath-alcohol test. He was seriously wounded and admitted to hospital. The man was not armed and was regarded by his workmates and whanau as a quiet law-abiding citizen. Outrage was expressed all around the country and there was a media outcry. The young constable was not being threatened and was clearly in error. He faced the possibility of serious criminal charges.

However, while senior police were still considering the case and contemplating their options, the extended family of the young man made an impassioned public plea to let the matter rest. 'We've all suffered enough already,' said his mother, 'and we would simply like the matter to rest to enable healing to occur. There's no need to punish anyone further. The only thing we'd like to happen is for us to have a chance to meet the young constable and talk with him.'

We need to reflect on these options if we are to avoid creating urban jungles like many inner cities of the United States and Europe. This is what restorative justice is all about.

Retributive justice, which is based primarily on vengeance and punishment, does us all a grave disservice by perpetuating a high violent-crime rate and creating a nation more embittered and angry about the breakdown of law and order with each passing year.

The 1994 figures speak to this. Seven years after laws were enacted in Aotearoa resulting in the mandatory imprisonment of violent offenders (minimum two years' jail), and with a resulting record-breaking number being imprisoned, there was a rise of 25 percent in violent crimes reported during the previous year. What a failure of policy!

The millions of dollars we spend on building new prisons and maintaining our old ones, generally speaking, is money wasted. In no other area of state expenditure do public monies get less scrutiny in terms of positive effectiveness than in the area of penal policy.

Restorative Justice
We need to discover a philosophy that moves from punishment to reconciliation, from vengeance against offenders to healing for victims, from alienation and harshness to community and wholeness, from negativity and destructiveness to healing, forgiveness and mercy. That philosophical base is restorative justice.

A positive philosophy that embraces a wide range of human emotions, including healing, forgiveness, mercy and reconciliation, as well as sanction where appropriate, has much to offer. In New Zealand the Children, Young Persons and Their Families Act 1989 has shown that a restorative rather than a retributive philosophy bears far better fruit, but such a process is a relatively new development for modern times. Howard Zehr, an international expert in the field of criminal justice, writes:

> Throughout most of Western history, crime has been understood as an offence of one person against another person, much like other conflicts and wrongs which are treated as 'civil'. Throughout most of this history, people have assumed that the central response must be to somehow make things right; restitution and compensation were very common, perhaps normative. Crime created obligations, liabilities, that needed to be taken care of, usually through a process of negotiation. Acts of vengeance could occur, but not, it appears, as frequently as is usually assumed and the functions of vengeance may have been different to what we expect. Both victim and offender had a responsibility in this process, as did the community. The state had a role as well, but it was limited and was by necessity responsive to the wishes of victims.
>
> This is a gross simplification, of course, but to some extent our history has been a dialectic between two modes of justice: state justice and community justice. State justice was imposed justice, punitive justice, hierarchical justice. Community justice was negotiated justice, restitutive justice.
>
> State justice has operated in some form during most of Western history. However, community justice predominated until fairly recently. Only in the past few centuries did state justice win out. The state won a monopoly on justice, but only with a great fight. The victory of state justice constituted a legal revolution of tremendous import, but a revolution which has been recognised and studied too infrequently. It is no accident that the birth of prisons – a new technology for delivering doses of pain – coincided with this legal revolution.[1]

Restorative justice is really not new. Biblical justice was restorative. So too was justice in most indigenous cultures. In pre-colonial New Zealand, Maori had a fully integrated system of restorative justice that used Maori legal processes. Many argue that the Treaty of Waitangi guaranteed its continuance. It was the traditional philosophy of Pacific nations such as Tonga, Fiji and Samoa: restorative justice was 'the Pacific way'.

In pre-Norman Ireland, restorative justice was interwoven very successfully with the very fabric of daily life. There were no police, sheriffs or public prisons. The decisions of the law were executed by the people concerned, supported by a highly organised and disciplined public opinion springing from honour and interest and inherent in the solidarity of the clan. There is good reason to believe that the system was as effective in the prevention and punishment of crime and in the redress of wrongs as any other human contrivance has ever been.[2]

The early chapters in this book will look specifically at the abysmal failure of the retributive system to administer justice fairly. The latter chapters provide insights as to how other cultures and traditions have fared under a restorative system, with emphasis on those near home: Maori, Samoan and Australian Aboriginal.

The concept of restorative justice is also widely known in other parts of the world. At a NATO advanced research workshop in April 1991 in Italy, papers were presented on various dimensions of restorative justice from Britain, Germany, the United States, Japan, Norway, Finland, New Zealand, Holland, Austria, France, Italy, Greece and Turkey. Not all of these countries are moving at the same pace to research the possibilities, but all are debating at various levels the shortcomings of a purely retributive justice system and the hope engendered by a system based on a more holistic restorative philosophy.

The law imposed by the English, wherever they colonised, was the law always of a conquering empire. The English did to others what the Roman Empire had attempted with them – impose its own form of imperial law. In essence it was hierarchical and centralised. In criminal matters it was retributive in nature, vengeful and punishing in effect. The restorative indigenous law of Ireland, Africa, Asia, the Pacific and the Caribbean was crushed and replaced by the imperial law of empire.

This book poses a question to nations seeking freedom and independence from former colonial masters: should not the philosophy underpinning criminal law also be reviewed? If, as this book alleges, the retributive system of criminal justice imported with colonisation is proving to be as disastrous as the statistics demonstrate, should not a free and independent nation shrug off the worst of its features, particularly if a local indigenous model promised to work better?

This book argues that the very ancient but very modern system of restorative justice would produce much more benefit for victims, offenders and society generally. Our resources and energies would be much better spent following such a philosophy. Do we really want to live in fear of criminals and violence? Many do already. Insecurity and fear are the dominant factors in their lives.

But that need not be. There are other ways: better ways, more positive and constructive ways, ways that will heal the hurt and pain of victims of crime using holistic and creative means. Why carry all that pain for a lifetime when, if the opportunity were provided, it could be dealt to and integrated into our lives? The results would lead to healing and peace of mind and a resumption of normal life.

It cannot happen under the present retributive criminal justice system. It could happen for many under a restorative one.

Footnotes

1. Howard Zehr, *Justice: the Restorative Vision*, Mennonite Central Committee, US Office of Criminal Justice, 1989
2. Encyclopaedia Britannica, Vol. 4, Encyclopaedia Britannica Ltd, London, 1959, p86

SECTION ONE

Retributive Justice

Each year jails take large numbers of hopeless people
and turn them into bitter hopeless people.

Time, 28 June 1993

CHAPTER ONE

Retribution: a Dead-end Street

Wayne, one of four children, was only five years old when he first got into trouble. He ran away from home and hid in a vacant house from which he stole some food. His drug-addicted mother had already had a child die at birth and another from a preventable disease at three years of age. His father, also an alcoholic drug addict, had recently returned from yet another term of imprisonment for violent assault, burglary and assorted drug offences.

When I was called to the house, Wayne was in his bedroom crying from the hiding his father had given him. His parents were anxious about how to keep him at home in the future. His thrashing wasn't an issue with them – that was the way they usually dealt with the children when they were naughty. In their own way they really did care for him and realised that their own dysfunctional behaviour was largely responsible for his plight. They didn't really know where to turn for lasting help.

The family was caught in a vicious cycle of deprivation, violence and hardship, alleviated by drugs and alcohol when money allowed. The parents' solution to their own relationship problems was usually violent, either verbally or physically. Social Welfare's options were limited. They were, on occasion, appalled at the standard of lifestyle of the family, but rightly recognised the love, tenderness and bonding that was present when things were 'going right'.

At four years of age, Wayne's chances of a drug-free or jail-free life were already minimal. His models of adult behaviour all involved violence, drugs, alcohol, unemployment and struggle. While there were brief periods of real stability and joy in his childhood, they were few and far between.

There was no possibility of his mother becoming and remaining drug-free because there was no programme within 800 kilometres that could provide the means of her coming to terms with her addiction while remaining bonded to her children. The resources were simply not there. There were no social or community workers equipped to help her learn good parenting or support her on her 'bad days'. The only option she felt she had was to call social workers at the centralised

Social Welfare office where, because of their stress-filled caseloads and her frustrations, there was often conflict. There were no jobs for her husband, who could be an excellent and willing worker but was always perceived as an ex-convict – obvious from the tattoos – and a drug addict as well. Rarely can such people find employment.

Wayne drifted through school, became bored by the age of 10, was caught stealing at the age of 11, and ended up in Social Welfare custody at 13 years of age. Now in his early twenties, he is a drug addict, has become an expert burglar, and is currently serving six years' imprisonment for the aggravated robbery of a service station. He went to jail on this sentence at the age of 17.

In order to survive he has grown devious and cunning. He is liable to emerge from prison a skilled safe-cracker, car thief and drug dealer, with a network of contacts that equals that of the 'old school tie' brigade. The taxpayers have already spent $400,000 on his tertiary 'education'. If he doesn't die violently by the time he is 30 years old – and there is a good chance he will – the government will probably have spent another $500,000 on incarceration fees. By that stage imprisonment will have harmed him almost beyond repair.

Because of stories like this, the New Zealand Catholic Bishops' Conference in 1987 described imprisonment as 'a poison in the bloodstream of the nation'. They called it an affront to human dignity, responsible for destroying, partially or totally, temporarily or permanently, those confined. They found it hard to imagine a more destructive or wasteful method of spending public funds.

The bishops were being cautious in their assessment. It is more than that. It is a deadly virus that contaminates all those associated with it. Despite the best efforts of some good staff and the positiveness of a percentage of inmates, the boredom, tedium, violence, waste, oppressive structures – the sheer inhumanity of the prison system – leaves its mark on all.

The system creates, and then exists within, a sub-culture all of its own. Few who spend any time in it ever fully recover from its negative effects on their lives. It changes people forever, and usually for the worse. Despite being well primed for it by his home life, Wayne is yet another victim of its voracious appetite.

The slim hope that he has is that the grace of God will yet intervene in his life and help him turn it around. That intervention could come in the form of a suitable habilitation programme with components that will help him face life drug- and alcohol-free, and help provide work-skill attributes that can lead him to paid employment as well.

Maybe the love of a good sensible partner will aid him in the process. It would certainly mean a tough transformation for him from the almost total self-centredness that survival and addiction have demanded to an appreciation of others. To love appropriately will be a learning process for Wayne and will not come easily, but it is still clearly possible. He will have to learn that love involves a lot more than sex.

For all that, Wayne's future appears bleak. It has been bleak right from the time he was a baby. He didn't seek drug-addicted, alcoholic, violent, unemployed parents. But to these he was born, and it is from that starting point that he must advance in life. However, the unevenness of this playing field makes it extremely difficult for him to ever catch up. He has a bigger handicap than a horse trying to win a Melbourne Cup carrying 100kg, or a New Zealand Cup starting off with a handicap of 150 metres. Even Cardigan Bay would not have been able to do it. The very best that Wayne can hope for is to keep touch with the pace and not get too far behind. The glittering prizes our culture holds before us as the rewards of success will never fall his way.

Any debate on social justice, law and order, crime and punishment, prisons and their effects, must always be placed in the wider social context of the society in which the debate occurs. There are cultural, economic and social influences abroad that markedly influence the type of crime committed, the levels of order and social control, the type of criminal justice system a nation has, and the role of imprisonment within that society.

For example, for widespread fraud you could be executed, or receive a heavy fine or a community-based sentence. The penalty handed down would depend on whether you lived in China or a modern capitalist Western nation. The difference in treatment flows from the culture of the people, and the ideology and rule of law imposed by its governing powers.

Most law is determined by culture and ideology. The ideology of the governing powers in Aotearoa/New Zealand is that of corporate capitalism, dominated by a particular type of monetarist capitalist ethic called the New Right. This ideology flows from a narrow consumer model of economics that allows 'market forces' to determine the various levels at which people may participate in society, contribute to it, and benefit from it.

In 1987 the Ministerial Committee of Inquiry into Violence in New Zealand produced a frightening indictment of our consumer culture. The report concluded that:

> We have the sort of society we deserve. For the past two or three decades permissiveness has gone unchecked, domestic violence is rampant, the macho image has been encouraged by advertising for commercial gain to the detriment of women, and aggressive behaviour and violence in sport have become accepted.[1]

The same violence that was analysed and condemned in 1987 is still found every day in our homes, on our streets, in our communities. It flows from a culture dedicated to the acquisition of material goods and money at the expense of practically everything else. Wayne, and a majority of imprisoned people like him, never receive the rewards that society offers achievers because too often they are handicapped out of the race by the social structures in which they live.

Penal Policy

Where does crime fit into this scenario? Sarah Van Gelder, an American sociologist, suggests root causes that lead to much criminal offending:

> Crime comes about when the underpinnings of our culture fail, when the ties that hold us together, socialise our children, and satisfy our needs are broken. Just as the environmental crisis reflects our failure to act in mindfulness of the interdependence of the human species and the other living creatures of the Earth, crime reflects our blindness to the fundamental interconnectedness of people.
>
> The result of this uprooting and neglect is that the solid core of contributing adult members crumbles, and the institutions that provide the foundations of community fall apart. The community safety net is left tattered. Parents, exhausted by long hours required to make ends meet or demoralised by their inability to cope with the hardships of poverty, may turn to drugs and alcohol. Kids are left on their own in what Elliot Currie calls 'adultless communities'.[2]

The end result of breeding generations of socially dysfunctional children is the breakdown of acceptable social mores and patterns of behaviour. Crime and violence result. At the heart of our means of control of such violence we have a philosophy of retribution, vengeance and punishment. These people will all be punished more. We are a punitive people and we are now being forced to live with the fruits of our desire for revenge. At the centre of our punitive obsession is the prison system upon which we spend hundreds of millions in a single year.

In the current system all power is given over to the state – judges, police, prison wardens. Victims and offenders are left feeling powerless; victims because they are shut out of the 'justice process' right from the beginning, and offenders because they are not offered the opportunity to take any real responsibility for their behaviour and actions. Instead, the orientation is merely to punish and the twin notions of taking responsibility and making things right again are ignored. Victims and offenders are denied power and accountability.

Punishment

The aim of good law is to build a strong, safe, healthy and just society. In dealing with crime, punishment or 'just desserts' must be in proportion, must contain a message of denunciation or moral censure, and must provide protection to the community and reparation to the victims.

This book argues that, for two reasons, none of these ideals is being achieved in the current retributive system. One reason is that our social structures are so inherently unjust that achieving such ideals is impossible without social transformation. The other is that the current criminal justice system focuses primarily on punishment.

The basic assumption about the relationship between criminal justice and punishment needs to be re-examined. Punishment is the deliberate infliction of suffering: it is legal violence. This book claims that punishment is counter-productive and needs fresh examination, as does the system that perpetuates it. This system is revealed as an emperor with no clothes. The idea that it can be reformed is a myth. That it is the only or best way of dealing with offenders is not true.

Let's take an illustration. Most big white-collar fraudsters are on bail until sentencing date, are given almost automatic minimum status within the prison system, and are released at the earliest possible date – usually after one-third of their sentence. On the other hand, blue-collar drug-addicted burglars, who usually have done much less social harm, are often remanded in custody until sentence, remain in medium-secure conditions while in jail (fewer privileges, worse prison conditions), and serve two-thirds of the sentence imposed.

In both cases, the punishment inflicted not only fails to achieve positive change in the offenders but guarantees a high chance of re-offending. It does not treat people fairly, gives a muddied message of moral censure (gross white-collar crime can be very profitable), provides no reparation to the victims, and only partially protects the community. Repeat offending upon release will be inevitable and will encompass fresh victims.

Punishment has become something the dominant group in society imposes on the those of little status and power who are not in a position to challenge its fairness or its usefulness. The political authorities are seen to be doing something about crime, but because what they are doing is counter-productive and actually a cause of more offending, crime rates continue to climb and more and more disempowered people get caught in its net.

The adversarial legal system spawned by the logic of punishment, as Canadian criminal justice consultant Lorraine Berzins says:

> ...is actually destructive of some of justice's most cherished objectives: the shared sense of what is right and wrong, the holding to account for wrongdoing, the affirming of the importance of the rights of the person injured, the sense of proportionality to the gravity of the misconduct, and the prevention of further harm.
>
> Today, the legal industry turns the search for justice into a game of technicalities played between lawyers in court. The central focus is that a law has been broken. This message overrides the victim's priorities and considerations, as well as any other rational concern for protection, rehabilitation

and ultimate healing of the relationship with the victim or the community. The entire symbolic message of denunciation must be carried by the length of prison sentence that is broadcast in headlines to the rest of the community.[3]

Imprisonment breaks down social personality and disempowers people. The vast majority of prison inmates become more self-centred and dependent on others during their time in prison. When one's world is reduced to a 3m by 2m cell and survival becomes the driving instinct, self-interest and self-centredness become major preoccupations.

Food becomes a primary concern and mealtimes become the focal point of waking hours. Life is trivialised. Mortgages, the kids, employment, your relationship with your spouse or partner, the depleting ozone layer and the nuclear threat are replaced as the major issues by the quality of the food, the amount of television viewing allowed, and the body odour of your cell-mate.

Imprisonment distorts and twists the psyche and the spirit of the imprisoned. For those already disturbed when they arrive, it aggravates their condition. Imagine a rapist sent to prison for 10 years lying day after day, night after night in a cell, dwelling on sexual fantasy and distorted visions. Imprisonment simply reinforces twisted thinking and unreal expectations of life. For many it guarantees more serious re-offending, which means more victims, more hurt, more pain and, for some, more terror.

It also has a destructive impact on innocent family members. Can anyone who has not experienced it have any idea of the horrific effect imprisonment has on family life? The impact is often horrendous when a principal adult figure is removed from the family. Children may lose a father or mother, parents a son or daughter. They are often then farmed out to relatives or the state for the duration of the sentence.

Alternatively, a spouse is left to survive as a single parent. Whatever strains existed in the relationship before the sentence are exacerbated by it, often to breaking point. The family is thrown onto a state benefit, which these days is often not enough to survive upon adequately. The model of adulthood placed before growing impressionable children is that of dad or mum who is a prisoner, a bad person, a jailbird, a convict.

Even visiting your loved one in prison is impossible for some. Most prisons in New Zealand are situated in the country and transport services are infrequent, if they exist at all. It's not hard to imagine the struggle some spouses must go through to bring themselves and their children out to see mum or dad between certain limited hours on a Saturday. This occurs week after week, often with little or no spare money or wider family support. Then there are the children at school – who is there to help them young people cope with the ignominy of having a parent in jail?

Former prison inmate Mike Martin writes:

> Prison may change people, it may cause some to be more crafty, but because of its punitive nature it is incapable of turning them into anything other than a lifetime liability to society.
>
> It is the very structure of penal policy that reinforces the inadequacies that lead to a criminal lifestyle in the first place. The more we elect to hide our small social problems behind high walls, the more deeply entrenched will be the problems that led people there. Worse than that is the fact that the offspring of our current jail population will soon follow in their parents' footsteps.
>
> Prisons cater to a public need: a need based on fear and ignorance; a desire to punish through retribution. It doesn't have to be that way, in fact such an attitude is little more than a mass cop-out. What we have developed after 100 years of penal policy is a vast and costly delaying mechanism. Imprisonment is used to delay confronting the real problems facing the community: it stops (for a while) an offender indulging in more crime; it delays social progress. It offers a breather and gives us a chance not to think about how to deal with the additional problems that will face the inmate on release.
>
> For 'justice' to mean anything, it must extend beyond a punitive reaction to an unacceptable action. Justice must mean much more than simply transferring a criminal from general society to a hidden society. The present method of justice is compounding the alienation of each individual. It is bonding people together within the source of their alienation.[4]

The great majority of prisoners are not murderers, rapists or desperate villains. They are ignorant young men under 30 who have failed at school or have been failed by school, and have no strong family or community links with anybody of sense. Their offences relate mainly to drink, drugs and cars. They are limited in their understanding of the difference between right and wrong and are in urgent need of education in every way. We, for our own future protection, are in urgent need that they should be educated.[5]

Many would argue that we have lost sight of the moral base underpinning both the law and our criminal justice system. As a result the aims of both are no longer clear to all. It is appropriate then to reflect on both law and morality if we are to ever recover or develop a social system that is clear in its objectives and fair to all.

Law and Morality

We are a nation with Western Judaeo-Christian traditions. This has had enormous impact on our social institutions, none more so than the law. Interpretations of scripture and the teachings of the Church from the 13th century on have helped shape the body of law we have inherited and our understanding of it.

Law has two dimensions, moral and legal. It is built on morality and is never neutral, always reflecting a system of values. Justice, truth, honesty, compassion and respect for people are the basic tenets of an acceptable morality that should seek to protect and enhance the common good.

Law and justice then are, regrettably, not synonymous terms. The law is not sacrosanct and never should be. What is sacrosanct is true justice, the dignity and equality of people, and respect for the human person over and above every other consideration.

In a secular society, good law and justice have to have the protection and enhancement of the common good as their starting point. Problems arise when the law is written by powerful interest groups with little feeling for the common good. This is the basis for unjust law, and the laws of apartheid were a stark illustration of this. It is worth noting that in countries such as the United States, Australia, Britain and New Zealand strong sectional interests have also had a major input into legislation; sometimes, it would seem, with scant regard for the common good. Good government should define, defend and protect the common good, particularly when there is a conflict of interest. This is precisely what Parliament in a true democracy should be about.

The promotion of the common good – that is, the good of the many as it is appreciated and understood by the majority – is at the heart of a fair and just moral code and central to the creation of good law. If the common good is to be achieved, our Judaeo-Christian heritage still has a special contribution to make. This religious tradition demands that the poor, the sick, the dispossessed and vulnerable minorities be especially protected. International covenants such as the United Nations Declaration of Human Rights and, in Aotearoa, the Treaty of Waitangi, seek to provide the same protection.

In our society this provision has clearly been eroded and massive injustice has resulted. The fruits of that injustice are everywhere. Poverty, racism and street kids are just three of many symptoms. The very fabric of our society is being strained and nowhere are its effects being felt more than in the criminal justice system.

I no longer believe that the retributive philosophy underpinning our criminal justice system can always offer a fair and just way of practising law. It no longer gives people justice in anything like the sense outlined above. Too often it fails to protect the common good. Certainly the poor more than anyone else get hammered by it. An adversarial court system that seeks to win regardless of the facts is just one blind spot in it. Its enormous costs in both human and financial terms are others. The elimination of victims from its central equation is another.

A philosophy primarily based on negative features such as punishment and vengeance is creating throughout the world a monster the likes of which will make the next century a living hell of fear of crime for a large portion of the world's people. It already is for many people in large cities.

As Howard Zehr says:

> Retributive justice defines justice the Roman way, as right rules, measuring justice by the intention and the process ... All action is hierarchical, from the top down. The state acts on the offender, with the victim on the sidelines ... Retributive justice as we know it views everything in purely legal terms. As Nils Christie has said, legal training is trained tunnel vision. In law school you are taught that only legally defined issues are relevant.[6]

We have failed to address the shortcomings of the retributive system and accept why it has proved to be such an abject failure in terms of addressing rising crime rates, the rights of victims, and the health and wellbeing of the community. A philosophy built on negativity can only produce negative results.

We should have learnt from the German experience. Professor Christian Pfeiffer, speaking at a conference in Perth, reported that 20 years ago West Germany had a sharp 50 percent increase in the use of imprisonment, with the inmate level rising to nearly 50,000 in 1983. From then on there was a sharp decline. Why did this happen?

The nation at the time was indulging in prison reform. The Social Democratic government, which came to power in 1972, had as one of its goals the reform of the prison system. They sought to make the system rehabilitative – really useful to society – and to educate young offenders in the institutions so as to make them better people afterwards. They passed legislation, built more prisons and invested a lot of effort in employing more social workers and psychologists.

This approach completely failed. Despite all the effort there was no change in the re-offending rate. Research on young offenders found 44 percent were unemployed when they entered prison and 66 percent were unemployed half a year after release, despite a lot of job training and meaningful activities while they were in prison.

Why did it happen? Because society does not accept ex-prisoners, and the inmates were insecure knowing that. They were theoretically prepared for the job market, but ill-prepared for the negative response they received from society. The recidivism rate remained at around 90 percent both before and after the new approach.

So the Germans changed tack: mediation within the community became the new approach. They used the insights of modern criminology to create varying non-custodial sentencing options. A wide range of community justice programmes were introduced, which, rather than seeking to punish offenders, sought to develop their life skills, self-esteem and sense of responsibility. Judges were urged to use fewer remands in custody and sentences of imprisonment. Research into judges' sentencing patterns revealed that 20 percent of judges were responsible for 50 percent of the jail sentences, so these judges were encouraged to change.

Prosecutors were urged to use their discretion and dismiss more cases where diversion was applicable or prosecution less warranted. New prison construction was halted, and widespread reparation was introduced.

Within a few years imprisonment numbers had been reduced by 20 percent throughout Germany, and in some cities, such as Berlin, by more than 50 percent. In the same period crime rates dropped significantly and the re-offending rate was reduced substantially.[7]

It is interesting to note that in Japan police, prosecutors and judges share an overriding mission to correct rather than punish, incapacitate or rehabilitate. American law professor John Haley, whose special expertise is Japanese law, reports that from the initial police interrogation to the final judicial hearing or sentencing, the vast majority of those accused of criminal offences confess, display repentance, negotiate for their victim's forgiveness and submit to the mercy of the authorities.

In return they are treated with extraordinary leniency, gaining at the very least the prospect of having their case dropped from the formal process altogether. To justify such leniency, law-enforcement officials must be satisfied the offender and the community are working together to compensate the victim and restore peace. Offenders' families become involved and, with the community, accept responsibility to ensure that steps will be taken to prevent further misconduct and provide some means of control. In addition, the victim must express forgiveness.[8]

The Japanese statistics are compelling. It is estimated the police do not report up to 40 percent of all apprehended offenders. Of those reported, prosecutors suspend up to one-third of all cases. For those who get to court, judges suspend sentences in nearly 60 percent of adjudicated cases. Only a fraction of offenders go to prison. Japan's imprisonment rate is 37 per 100,000 population, or about one-quarter the New Zealand rate. The most recent studies of recidivism indicate that the more lenient the treatment of offenders, the less likely the offender is to commit another offence within three years.

Perception versus Reality

If this is the case, then there is obviously a massive gap between public perception of how to deal with crime and the reality. There is also a huge gap between what people perceive to be the level of crime in the community and the real level. Here the media play a crucial role.

In October 1994 a young woman in South Carolina named Susan Smith spoke tearfully of the anguish she was enduring as a result of her two children being abducted. On nationwide television she begged for their return, claiming that a masked black man had been responsible. In South Carolina, a former slave state, that claim touched a deep nerve among white residents. The nation was stunned at the callousness of the act. Yellow ribbons, signs of hope and a safe return, were wrapped around trees. Candle-lit prayer vigils were held throughout the land. Mass media carried her story around the world, and President Clinton made a special statement. Dozens interviewed on television spoke of their insecurity regarding their children, and wondered out loud what was happening to America. It was no longer a safe place to bring up kids. Who would be next?

Then the facts emerged. The children were dead and their mother had killed them. After nine days, Susan Smith was arrested and charged with double murder. But the perception portrayed by the media of an unsafe, insecure environment for children will long remain etched into the scarred emotional tissue of the nation.

People in the United States should feel the safest in the world. In 25 years, since 1968, in order to make themselves safer and feel more secure, they have increased their prison population by a whopping 700 percent. Yet do Americans feel any more secure as a result? No way, it seems. In 1994 they voted to double that rate again within the next decade. Will they feel safer and more secure then? I fear the answer will still be no.

The same policy has been followed in New South Wales. There, the upping of the hype by politicians calling for harsher penalties in the early part of this decade resulted in a massive 60 percent increase in imprisonment and the construction of five new prisons. Next door in the state of Victoria, where the crime rate is virtually the same but where there was no political hype, the imprisonment rate remained constant at about half the NSW rate.

This trend is all about public perception and has little, if anything, to do with reality. To tackle the causes of crime and deal with the causes of criminal offending requires a much more mature, informed response. But public fear sells newspapers, raises TV ratings and gets politicians elected. It leaves the rest of us with a legacy of a continued high crime rate, insecurity and financial indebtedness.

The media, especially television, must take some responsibility for the distorted perception they present of crime in the community. It fuels public fear and insecurity, which in turn tend to influence politicians in their legislative role and judges in their sentencing. How often does the television news start its presentation with two or three crime stories, one after the other? An armed hold-up here, a sex offender sentenced there, and a shoot-out in Miami or Rome to bring an international dimension. This type of 'news' has become part of the daily television diet, beamed into family home across the country.

Who gains from such coverage? Only the television companies, the advertisers and the titillated. Often the police have had to remind us, after saturation coverage of a particularly nasty crime, that this is still a safe country to live in.

It's not that the stories are necessarily inaccurate, (though it is difficult to see how much balance one can get in a 15-second 'bite'). It's the portrayal of society that is the most distorted. Listening to talkback radio shows how distorted the public perception of crime is. Seeing crime stories every day leads people to feel that the community is full of criminals waiting to attack. That is simply not true.

Conclusion

Retributive justice is a philosophy that is bankrupt. Just how bankrupt it is will be clearly seen in the following four chapters, which look at its effect in New Zealand, Britain, Australia and the United States. It no longer offers any positive contribution to the wellbeing of communities or the development of a just social fabric for society. As Christchurch lawyer Wolfgang Rosenberg says, '…the public cry for retribution shows that we are still close to barbarism. Civilisation begins when vendetta ends.'

Its deformed stepchild, the prison system, is an even bigger evil. Prison is a dead-end street. Socially, morally, financially and spiritually, it is a cancer eating away at the heart of the human community. It is as evil and obsolete as slavery. While most acknowledge the need for a few dangerous offenders to be kept locked away from society, such offenders need to be kept in a positive, constructive, secure environment where they are still treated with respect.

For the rest there are creative, community-based alternatives, including a wide range of city, urban and marae-based habilitation centres. The 1989 Prison Systems Review headed by a former High Court judge, the late Sir Clinton Roper, recommended more community work options and employment schemes. These, the review said, should be coupled with genuine preventative programmes such as parenting groups, co-operative neighbourhood work schemes, more free adult education courses, and the development of good local health-care programmes.

The millions of dollars wasted so sinfully on the prison system could be freed up to provide the resources necessary to attack crime at its very roots, thus preventing its development and escalation.

Footnotes

1. Report, Ministerial Committee of Inquiry into Violence, Government Print, Wellington, 1987
2. Sarah Van Gelder, 'The Ecology of Justice', *In Context* No 38
3. Lorraine Berzins, article in the *National Prison Project Journal*, Spring 1993
4. Mike Martin, *NZ Listener*, 22 June 1985
5. *Sunday Times* (UK), 1 May 1994
6. Howard Zehr, *IARCA Journal*, International Association of Residential and Community Alternatives, March 1991
7. Professor Christian Pfeiffer, paper 'Criminal Justice: An Alternative View', from the conference 'Prison, the Last Option', 18-19 October 1991, published by the Anglican, Catholic and Uniting Church of Australia
8. John Haley, *Crime and Justice Network Newsletter*, Mennonite Central Committee, Pennsylvania, September 1991

CHAPTER TWO

New Zealand Criminal Justice: A Punitive Obsession

> The evil of our prison system is that not only are our prisons generating more criminal activity, but they are promoting crime.
>
> *Peter Williams Q.C.*

In May 1993 an 80-year-old Auckland man, Jack Maaka, was sentenced in the Auckland District Court to six months' imprisonment for benefit fraud. The sentence for this World War II veteran was confirmed by a High Court judge on appeal.

The sentence came in a week that saw the Minister of Justice, Doug Graham, and the head of the Justice Department's criminal justice section, Mel Smith, calling for imprisonment to be used only as last resort.[1] It was a sentence that highlighted the punitive nature of New Zealand society and the inability of the judiciary and courts to look beyond their tunnel vision to see what is appropriate and what is not in sentencing options.

That New Zealand is a punitive society can become very clear to anyone listening to a radio talkback session any day of the week. Mel Smith says that as a society we are more puritanical than, for example, Australians, and we prosecute people for a wide range of behaviour ignored overseas. He says there is more reporting of crime in New Zealand and our police force is better at catching offenders. Criminals who a few years ago attracted fines are now being sent to periodic detention, often because they cannot pay. The next time they offend, they end up in prison. They can, and should be, dealt with outside the prison system.[2]

Doug Graham agrees. He says our imprisonment rates are higher because we live in a society that exacts revenge. People are more interested in revenge than in some other elements of criminal justice.[3]

The Jack Maaka sentence is a classic case of a retributive sentence. The man's age, his war record, his mana in the Maori community and his explanation that he believed he was entitled to the extra monies because of his wartime service were all taken into account by the sentencing judge, who commented on all these things. But the best the retributive system had to offer was six months in Mt Eden Prison.

Imprisonment violates the most basic of human rights, yet daily judges send off dozens to serve time in them. And they do it on behalf of the community. We too are responsible for this situation.

Aotearoa has an horrendous record, second only to the United States in the Western world, in the number of people we imprison. This despite official policy in recent years to reduce the number. Successive ministers and secretaries of justice have called for a lowering of the imprisonment rate. As long ago as 1980, the Minister of Justice, Jim McLay, and the Secretary of Justice, John Robertson, promoted a public campaign to reduce our exorbitant rate, which was already being quoted as one of the highest in the world. Yet the rate has soared throughout the 1980s and 1990s, way beyond any other reasonable rate in the Western world.

The fact that our imprisonment rate has grown out of all proportion to the number of offences being committed exacerbates the problem. It highlights the lack of political will by successive governments and by the Justice Department to change this trend.

They should have recognised the opportunities offered by the 1989 Prison System Review of Sir Clinton Roper and his team and created a parallel system of sanction that dealt to the causes of offending. A nationwide series of habilitation centres would have been already producing the fruits of their endeavours and, if Justice Department figures are anything to go by, would have been reducing re-offending.

> The evidence suggests that well-run treatment programmes for some types of criminal offenders can reduce the incidence of re-offending substantially. Given good conditions, reductions in reconvictions of 15-20 percent can be expected.[4]

Instead, six years after the report, we are still awaiting the first pilot schemes.

All the indications are that there is very little political will to grapple realistically with crime and its consequences. Instead, a 19th-century rationale and process remains at the heart of the nation's response.

New Zealand politicians simply do not take crime seriously. For too many their tub-thumping, emotive, vote-catching spiels reflect ignorance and prejudice rather than intelligent comment. If the politicians did take crime seriously, they would have developed a pan-party national strategy to hit the causes of so much offending – male violence, drug and alcohol addiction, unemployment, sexual aberration, spiritual and cultural alienation, motor-car addiction.

We imprison at a rate of 130 per 100,000 population. Queensland jails at a rate of 71, Victoria 51, Ireland 44, Holland 39, the Philippines 22. In 1981 we jailed

3531 adults. This figure had grown to 8228 by 1991, which is an increase of 223 percent.[5]

When it comes to numbers within the wider corrections system, including periodic detention and community services, New Zealand is way ahead of any Australian state and all of the above-mentioned countries with a whopping 756 people per 100,000 of population. This is despite the fact that the rate of offending in Aotearoa has been similar to and sometimes lower than that in these other states and countries.

We imprison far more and it is costing us heaps: around $260 million annually. Some 3000 staff are needed to provide round-the-clock surveillance. Yearly costs per inmate in 1993 varied from $24,000 for those on prison farms to $67,000 for those in maximum security, an average of around $40,000 per inmate.[6]

The truth of the matter is that many offenders who in New Zealand go to jail, would receive community-based sentences elsewhere. And many offenders who receive community-based sentences here, especially periodic detention, would receive fines or a non-supervisory sentence elsewhere.

The New Zealand criminal justice system has close to the largest number of people per capita under its control of any Western nation. As Minister of Justice Doug Graham said in a speech in 1991:

> The probability is that if prison sentences in the vast majority of cases were halved, the crime rate would not increase and the public would be no less safe.[7]

All the evidence is that long prison sentences and increased prison numbers do not lower crime rates. The number of New Zealanders in prison has increased every year since 1980, the population level has remained reasonably static at 3.3 million people, yet the crime rate has soared.

The Justice Department report to Parliament in 1993 said that despite the prison muster rise and harsher mandatory sentences, imprisonment numbers and crime continued to increase. The report also said the department was convinced that the continued use of prison sentences was not succeeding in reducing crime.

This confirms all the overseas research, which shows exactly the same pattern. For example, in Texas, Nevada and Florida, where the imprisonment rate is higher and sentences longer than anywhere else in the United States, the crime rate is approximately the same as in states such as Minnesota and Hawaii, where the imprisonment rate is one-fifth to one-quarter the size.[8]

Sociologist Greg Newbold believes that tough prisons produce tough citizens who are dangerous inside or outside prison. He quotes figures from the United States to show that harsher penalties and tighter security in jails leads to higher crime rates. In 1986 the average sentence for robbers was four years' imprisonment. By 1991 it had risen to seven and a half years. Yet there was no real sign of a reduction in the number of robberies being committed.

Since 1976, when capital punishment was re-introduced, largely as a deterrent, homicides have increased from 16,600 per year to more than 20,000, and death rows in most states are bulging. The implication is that the tougher we make prisons and the longer we make sentences, the greater will be the crime rate and the more horrendous the nature of some of the crimes committed.[9]

We are set to build even more prisons in the 1990s to meet the expected demand. More than 1000 extra cells may be needed by 1996.[10]

Imprisonment: the Facts

There are several facts that need to be noted about imprisonment.

1. The Poor Go to Prison

The 1981 Penal Policy Review of Mr Justice Casey put it starkly:

> Most offenders are disadvantaged, handicapped emotionally or spiritually, immature or merely stupid. Very few are motivated by what moralists of the older generation would call 'the forces of evil'.[11]

According to the Justice Department a pen portrait of the average inmate goes like this:

> Aged 27, three-quarters are single, divorced, separated or widowed. About two-thirds are beneficiaries, three-quarters unemployed, half have severe alcohol and/or drug problems (two-thirds of women inmates), half have had psychiatric assessment, half come from broken homes, nine out of 10 have no formal qualifications, and only a handful own their own homes or have significant assets. A little fewer than half are Pakeha, the rest Polynesian.[12]

This picture is the same in every similar country in the world. The poor, the dispossessed, the vulnerable, the sick and the addicted are those who fill our prisons.

Interestingly, even having a job with poverty-line wages is no guarantee that one can avoid imprisonment. A study undertaken in 1993 by Tony Short, senior law lecturer at the University of South Australia, showed that the employment contracts system had been a large contributor to New Zealand's having the worst crime rate in the industrialised world.

His report compared his research with a Dutch Justice Ministry study based on surveys in 1989 and 1992 among 55,000 people in 20 countries.[13] He concluded that the act was a significant cause of poverty and misery. It had succeeded in driving down wages in low-skill industries, which in turn had led to increased poverty and crime. Both reports found that the two were clearly linked.[14]

2. Imprisonment Increases Crime Rates

Prisons, long known as 'universities of crime', are a primary place to recruit new friends and new gang members, learn new criminal skills, plan new crimes. Much of the daily conversation among inmates involves bragging about what has been done in the past and what might be possible in the future. Many major crimes are performed by groups of ex-prison inmates who combine their various skills to perform the crime. Often they have been colleagues in prison. Fellow graduates.

Most of the horrific crimes of rape and murder committed in recent years have been carried out by ex-inmates. All prison did for them was harden them in their attitudes, make them more bitter, and set them up emotionally and socially to perform some horrendous act of violence. Upon release they became walking time-bombs.

Yet where is the public outcry at the abysmal failure rate of our prison system? Why are we not demanding some positive results? If the education or health system failed as regularly and made people less literate and more sick, the streets would be packed with demonstrators demanding value for their tax dollar. Why doesn't it happen for the criminal justice system? It has proven to be a total failure now for decades.

Such failed policies as the increased penalties of the 1980s have guaranteed some of the horrific crime of the 1990s. In 1982 only 18 percent of offenders (excluding traffic cases) were imprisoned or received periodic detention. By 1991 that figure had reached 39 percent. The number of convictions had not risen – what had risen was the rate of imprisonment and periodic detention as the means of sanction.[15]

Statistics show that most prison inmates are affected by one or other or all of the following problems: drug addiction, illiteracy, dyslexia, alcohol addiction, a propensity for violence, unemployment, poverty, the absence of a meaningful spirituality and the ethics and values that flow from it, self-hatred, sexual aberration. A high proportion of crime flows from the inability of the person to deal adequately with life because of the effects of one or other of these deficiencies.

For example, it has been estimated that up to 75 percent in some prisons cannot read and write well enough to cope with everyday aspects of life such as filling out forms or reading a newspaper. Yet there is growing evidence that when dyslexia, hearing problems and illiteracy are tackled, a dramatic change in the outlook on life results for the newly literate. Their self-esteem mushrooms, their confidence expands and there is a flow-on effect into other areas of life.[16]

More than 75 percent of inmates have a problem with alcohol or drugs or both. It stands to reason that if such cases were dealt with by adequate programmes backed by the substantial resources required, re-offending would drop. The fact that a parallel system of habilitation centres, some of which could have focused on drug and alcohol addictions, has yet to become a reality while an extra $180 million has been spent since 1989 on new prisons and upgrading old ones is indicative of where the Justice Department's priorities lie.

3. Imprisonment Brutalises People

It is difficult to assess just how damaged people can be by a prison sentence. For those who go immediately to new minimum-security facilities, the damage may be minimal. But for the majority who have to spend time in our larger institutions, prison life can brutalise. There are many ways this can happen.

Any notion of self-responsibility is abolished upon entry. You are there to do as you are told, when you are told. You lose most of the control of your life and its direction. Decisions are made, orders given, and a paramilitary-type structure implements the orders.

Your senses are under attack – by noise, by yelling from guards and inmates, by televisions and radios going at all hours of the day and into the night. You adapt and cope but are desensitised in so doing. Then there is the tedium and boredom, the real killers in our prison system. As Phil Berrigan says, it is a deadly abrasive that works upon a person's spirit like wind and water on loose soil. The erosion that results is very nearly inevitable. How depressing, he says, to see men of intelligence and accomplishment licking their wounds like punished children, feasting on distractions, and longing uncritically for a society that has misused them. Tedium feeds on drabness and routine. As such it is a real form of structural violence.[17]

Then there is the physical violence. One in six inmates is kept in a special wing away from others for fear of physical violence. The macho culture of the prison sees to it that few people escape its all-embracing effects. 'Control squads' of prison officers are designated in all major prisons to quell disturbances and violence. That we need them as part of a national policy is merely indicative of how violent prison can be.[18]

In February 1991 inmates smuggled reports out of Mt Eden Prison in Auckland that gave a picture of conditions among the worst in the country. For example, in East Block, a wing of the prison, they claimed the following constituted their daily routine and living conditions.

> Unlocked at 6am for 10 minutes to collect breakfast. Locked in cell until 8am. Spend time in the exercise yard. At 10am returned to the wing for showers, and lunch is served between 10.30 and 11am. Locked in the cell from 11am until 1pm. Locked in the yard from 1pm until 3.30pm, then returned to the wing and served dinner. Locked away until the next day to start the routine again. The total hours of lock-up are 18 out of 24 hours. All meals are eaten in the cell.

The cells are grim grimy concrete caves with two steel beds and a toilet. Poor natural lighting comes from a 50cm by 25cm barred window. Even during daylight on a sunny day the light has to be turned on to enable you to read. The floor of the cell is bitumen, a breeding ground for germs. The walls in most cells are filthy and the wiring in some of the cells is exposed and in a dangerous condition.

A cell is about the size of an average bathroom, and if you can imagine spending 18 hours a day in your bathroom, eating, sleeping and relieving yourself in the company of your cell-mate, you start to have an idea of what it is like. The difference is that the average bathroom is clean.

The exercise yard is a concrete compound with a lean-to at one end. In the corner of the lean-to is a toilet, urinal and cold-water shower, all open to the view not only of other inmates but of the officers who overlook the yards. Many of the officers are women. The other half of the structure has wooden benches and a TV set, where men huddle when it is windy or raining. Often it is standing room only. The only exercise equipment provided by the Justice Department is a plastic football.

At the moment the muster is 59 men. When we are let in for a shower at 10am, the water remains hot for about 10 minutes. There are six shower heads for the whole wing. On Mondays we have a change of underwear, and on Thursdays a full kit change. During kit change there always seem to be female officers present even if they have not been on duty in the wing during the day. The whole system is dehumanising and demoralising.[19]

The taxpayer invests over $40,000 a year on average per prisoner to keep this iniquitous situation in force.

4. Imprisonment Wrecks Relationships

Thousands of families have a partner torn from their midst and imprisoned every year in New Zealand. For the one imprisoned this means the heart-wrenching effects of being isolated from spouse and children, and the fear of never quite knowing what they are doing at any given time. For some there is a constant worry as to whether a partner is remaining faithful on the outside. 'Dear John' letters are not uncommon in prison. There is also the loss of employment for many upon their imprisonment

As noted earlier, for the families the break can be even harder. There is the stigma of having a spouse, a son or daughter, a brother, a partner, a sister in prison. There is the ignominy for some of having to be supported on state benefits. Being dependent on welfare is not everybody's cup of tea. There is the added stress of trying to maintain a relationship when contact is limited to one hour a week. For many, even getting to the prison is a difficulty since they have no transport and some of the larger prisons (Paremoremo, Rolleston, Paparua, Waikeria) are in rural areas. It is often the family who do the hardest part of the sentence.

5. Drugs in Prison

A drug-addicted veteran of the New Zealand prison system, writing in the magazine *Wide Appeal* (Issue Zero, February 1994), spoke of having used most drugs while doing time over 12 years, including everything from cannabis to morphine:

> I believe people use drugs in jail mainly to escape the reality of confinement. It is a mental state of escaping. When you are stoned on drugs in jail, you are in another reality that is not prison (hopefully!). A group of blokes that use drugs is often called 'the crew'. Getting stoned within the crew is an everyday thing. The crew live and breathe drugs. Drugs are their existence, their reality, their life. Without the use of drugs these inmates can become very depressed and angry. Hanging out for days is possibly more damaging than using. I have seen men nearly kill for drugs, and escape 'over the wall' in order to 'escape' again when they score.
>
> I have seen many dangerous situations where the inmate is too stoned to know what he is doing, where one crew is fighting another crew because one group has more dope than the other. To be part of a 'drug crew' may even be something other inmates look up to. Using syringes is common, yet there are very few syringes available. They are hard to obtain and have to be smuggled in. Sharing the 'gun' or the syringe becomes par for the course, so the Hepatitis C virus moves on and on and on!
>
> I have noticed over the years the number of inmates using drugs has risen alarmingly. Compared to 10 years ago, when there would be 35 percent using, now it's 90 percent using one form of drug or another. There is no way the Justice Department can stop drugs being brought into prison. If an inmate wants drugs then he will think of a way to get them. Due to cost-cutting in prisons there is very little treatment for drug users. If an inmate is released from prison with a drug habit, what start has he or she in society? They will only link up with their drug peers and the circle of offending will only continue.

One of the anomalies of imprisonment is that prison is the place where some inmates first get introduced to drugs. They go in clean and can come out drug addicts. That drugs are readily available in prisons is known by all who live and work in them. In January 1994, the MP for Wellington-Karori, Mrs Pauline Gardiner, herself a former drug counsellor, told of a former Christchurch inmate who ran up a $6000 drug debt while in prison. [20]

A 1992 Justice Department report found that over two-thirds of female inmates and roughly half of men in prison were identified as having some sort of problem with substance abuse. Drugs used most frequently were marijuana, tranquillisers and opiates. Just over two-thirds of the men and just over half of the women indicated they had not discussed or received any help for their substance abuse while in prison.

Fleur Grenfell, general manager of Arohata Prison, says it is not unusual for inmates to be introduced to drugs in prison.

I hate to see glue sniffers turning into needle users. But you put druggies together and that is what you are going to get.[21]

As for getting off drugs while in prison, for most it is impossible. Timaru-based alcohol and drug centre worker Debbie Martin pointed out to a Christchurch conference the difficulty of coming off drugs in jail.

Intravenous drug users who have a habit find they are unable to stop it if they go to jail and there is not always effective treatment for them. So they have continued to use drugs.[22]

The co-ordinator of Christchurch PARS, the Prisoners Aid and Rehabilitation Society, Kathy Dunstall, disclosed that PARS officers regularly see inmates and former inmates with debts of $200-300 for drugs brought in prison. Pressure could be exerted on inmates while they were in prison and after their release.

Inmates take drugs to escape the boredom of prison life, and some acquire their addictions while serving their sentence.[23]

The problem does not stop there. Pressure is often brought to bear on vulnerable partners and spouses of inmates by outside contacts of drug-selling prisoners to pay for jail drug debts. Threats and intimidation are not uncommon in securing such payment.

That drug addiction leads to further crime should come as no surprise. In a report to the Christchurch City Council in May 1994, the Narcotic Addiction Resource Group, which comprises professionals working in the field of drug addiction, claimed that drug-related crime by addicts waiting for places on the methadone treatment programme was costing Christchurch $13 million a year: about $250,000 a week.

6. Prisons Are Recruitment Grounds

There is no better recruitment area for criminal behaviour and gang and club membership than prisons. This is not necessarily always a negative thing. If a person is recruited by one of the more progressive and mature gangs or motorcycle clubs, then for the first time a young offender might find a sense of identity and self-esteem. More often, though, it is the heavy gangs, well into criminal activity, who do the most recruiting. The rise of 'white power' gangs in the community and of some of the more disreputable Maori and Polynesian groupings can be directly attributed in part to the time spent in prison by members.

For a person wishing to break his or her gang affiliations, prison can prove to be an impossible place to be. Many young men and women recruited as teenagers into gangs wish to break off their association as they mature, raise families and seek a different lifestyle. Prison reinforces gang affiliations and makes it extremely difficult for members wishing to make the break to do so.

7. Deterrence Is a Myth

One of the most frequent phrases heard from sentencing judges is that the sentence to be imposed will help deter other offenders. Every person working with offenders knows that to be simply a myth. It is a concept promoted by middle-class educated people about themselves. They are saying that the threat of imprisonment and exposure would deter others like them from offending.

Recently the rape sentence maximum was raised from 14 to 20 years. The change attracted a lot of publicity and most adults probably heard mention of it. Has this move slowed the pattern of rapes and attacks on women? Not if reports in the media give any indication. Such violence is as prevalent as ever.

In the period 1985-92 incidents of violent crime rose by 41 percent, despite a nearly two-thirds increase in the length of prison terms for such offences. Statistics in New Zealand also revealed a 3 percent decrease in overall crime figures in the year ended 30 June 1994. Many areas of criminal offending – traffic, fraud, burglaries, thefts – showed a marked drop in offending rates. The two areas where offending rose substantially against this national trend, violent crime and drug offending, were the two areas where penalties had increased most in the previous 10 years. The rationale behind increasing the penalties at the time was one of deterrence.[24]

Mike Martin, a man who has spent most of his adulthood in prison, writes:

> We must stop imposing sanctions on criminals simply because we think a particular form of punishment would deter us. We, that is you and those who represent you, are *not* the offender, so it is time you stopped believing the punishment that would deter you would also deter the average criminal. If anything the opposite is true.[25]

The recidivism rates tell it all. Nearly two-thirds come back to prison within two years of a sentence. Does the burglar think of prison when he or she goes out to burgle? Does the car thief? The rapist? The molester? The fraudster? The conman? Not if you listen to their stories. Being caught does not enter their calculations.

8. Prisons Are Expensive

Prisons are very expensive to run. There is real irony in the fact that after little enough is spent on some youngsters by way of education, health, clothing and shelter during their formative years, when they hit prison the state becomes extremely generous. The state will spend nearly $70,000 a year for a maximum-security prisoner, and between $24,000 and $35,000 for a minimum-security inmate. This breaks down to $1500 a week spent on each prisoner's care and upkeep for the length of a prison term, or about $200 a day.

Of course it will not all be spent on the inmate. In fact very little will be. From that sum, $1375 will be spent on the administration of the prison, mainly in the form of prison officer wages. The prisoner's food costs only $5-6 per day.

New Zealand now spends $150.8 million each year in running its prison system. Capital costs for new prison construction push this much higher. A proposed 1000 more cells by 1996 could cost $195 million, with an extra $22 million being added each year to the bill for running costs.[26]

Yet all over the country, the internal costs of running prisons are being cut back. While more and more cells and prisons are being built, the budgets to keep the current ones up and running are being slashed. The first things to go in prison budget-cutting are the food costs and programmes for prison inmates. For example, at Christchurch Women's Prison in 1993 all outside-supplied drug, alcohol and education programmes were cut because of 'severe financial constraints' imposed by government funding cuts.[27]

Alcohol and drug addiction therapy provided by Odyssey House, the Community Alcohol and Drug Service and Te Rito Arahi, a Maori drug programme, were cut. This left the inmates without professional drug and alcohol therapists despite the fact that 85 percent of the women have drug- and alcohol-related problems.

Ironically the same week these cuts were announced, Dr Julie Leibrich, the Justice Department Centennial Research Fellow, released a report that showed that criminals stop offending when they have something of value they do not want to risk. They change when they come to a personal decision that offending is no longer worthwhile.[28]

The most obvious way of helping inmates reach a level of self-awareness and confidence so that they really do come to value something in their own lives is through the very programmes axed by the prison management.

9. The Link between Crime and Unemployment

It is one of the most difficult things to prove, yet one of the most obvious facts of life, that high unemployment breeds an increase in crime rates. In 1972, 12 percent of people sentenced to prison, borstal or put on probation/parole were classed as unemployed. By 1987, along with the vast increase in crime and prison rates, that proportion had risen to 66 percent.[29]

Taken alone, these statistics tell us very little because of other mitigating circumstances. But placed alongside overseas research, they confirm the increased crime/unemployment links. It follows, for example, from Julie Liebrich's research that if a person is unemployed, feeling pretty lousy and not very useful, they are much more likely to offend. If they are employed on a reasonable wage, are treated decently and have something to work for, with a resultant development of self-esteem and confidence, they are less likely to offend.[30]

According to a report published in Britain in 1982, there is a striking relationship between unemployment and imprisonment levels. Researchers found that for every 1000 young people unemployed there are 56 more admissions to penal institutions. Higher unemployment means more crime and more imprisonment.[31]

Researcher M. H. Bremner found in both Britain and the United States that for every 1 percent rise in unemployment there was a 4 percent rise in prison admissions.[32]

A clear corollary follows. A government that stands back and allows market forces to determine unemployment levels becomes a co-respondent in the increase in crime that results. There is a clear link between government policy on unemployment (allowing market forces to prevail) and rising crime rates. One flows from the other. All things are interconnected.[33]

10. The Prison System Is Selective

If you are poor, under-educated, Maori or Polynesian, young, unemployed, unskilled or addicted to drugs or alcohol, you stand a very good chance of ending up in prison. Conversely, if you are educated, skilled, middle-class, Pakeha, employed, well paid and have stable family relationships, there is only a minute chance of its happening. It is not that the second groupings do not break the law on occasion. But the type of offending the former grouping engages in – assaults, minor drug possession and/or dealing, shoplifting, burglaries, thefts, driving offences – is far more highly policed and is the subject of much more media concern that the anti-social actions of their better-off compatriots.

As J. H. Reiman notes in his book *The Rich Get Richer and the Poor Go to Prison,* the criminal justice system does not protect us against the gravest threats to life, limb or possession. Its definitions of crime are not simply a definition of the objective dangers that threaten us. The workplace, the medical profession, the air we breathe and the poverty we refuse to rectify lead to far more human suffering, death and disability, and take far more from our pockets than murders, aggravated assaults and theft. As he says, this type of human suffering is preventable.

So too are unemployment, poverty, racism. And unfair taxation and the opulence of the few at the expense of the many. Yet such inequalities are protected by law in this country. We place individual human rights over and above any other consideration, including that of the common good. The result is that some families can live in packing cases in Auckland carparks while others can have holiday homes and city mansions for their private use. One person can own an island (created 10 million years before he was born) and prevent others from living on it. Another can own 300 homes for rental at any cost, while the law forbids squatting to the homeless family.

Conclusion

We are all responsible for the high crime rates and levels of imprisonment. Naturally offenders must take prime responsibility for their offending. Most make choices that place them outside the law. But successive governments, the Justice Department, and the judiciary are co-responsible with offenders for the high crime rate because of the inept way they have used their power in failing to build a more just society and a fairer criminal justice system.

The media also play a special role in distorting the public perception of the true state of offending in our society.

The Justice Department is basically empire-building, protecting its power base and control over the whole correctional field. What other explanation is there for its deliberate subversion of the of the central thrusts of the Roper Report, which recommended a parallel but separately controlled system of sanction? How else to explain their continued belief in the face of so much contradictory evidence that prisons can both punish and habilitate? How else to explain the cynical application of the word 'habilitate' to prison programmes when the report made it very clear that this was a new and fresh way of viewing things and was not a philosophy applicable to traditional prisons? They must be held co-responsible for continued high crime rates and imprisonment numbers.

Successive Ministers of Justice have failed when vision and moral courage was needed. Admittedly, things moved a little under both Geoffrey Palmer in his first term and under Doug Graham. But they have joined other Ministers in responding too rapidly with ill-conceived legislation involving harsher penalties whenever the well-orchestrated red-neck element mobilises. Their political parties have failed to think through the implications of continuing with a retributive philosophy of justice. Too many politicians have been happy to accept tired, disreputable arguments about penalties without seeing the ramifications for the wider community and what sort of society we are creating. Doug Graham has often brought a balance and a thread of wisdom to some of the emotional debates that rage periodically in the community. He seems to have failed to carry the rest of his party to the same conclusions.

The judiciary must be held to be co-responsible for this situation because of the entrenched harsh views of many judges on sentencing. No-one is suggesting that certain people should not be sentenced to imprisonment for certain offences. But the whole idea of the Criminal Justice Act 1985 was to keep people out of prison by expanding the range of community sentences. This was the will of Parliament. The act lays down clear guidelines to indicate that, apart from special circumstances, only violent offenders should be imprisoned. Yet at the time of the prison census in 1989 only 55 percent of inmates were there because of violent offending. As Doug Graham has said, the simple fact is that many people who receive prison sentences in New Zealand would receive community-based sentences in other countries.[34]

Sir Clinton Roper, speaking to Australian and New Zealand judges in 1990, said that in his view:

> ... the act had failed in its purpose, not through any fault in the philosophy behind it but in the failure of the courts to recognise and apply its principles.

Judges, so quick at times to pontificate about the will of Parliament when it comes to increasing prison sentences, have been too often too slow in reflecting the will of Parliament when it comes to alternative sentencing. The Crown has the right to appeal against the insufficiency of sentence and has a very high rate of success in so doing. As a result, a tariff of sentence has been set in many areas of crime by the Court of Appeal, which has severely curtailed the discretion of a sentencing judge.

This means an individual sentencing judge has his judicial discretion to grant a person a non-custodial sentence severely curtailed and this in itself contributes to the abnormally high number of people in New Zealand prisons.[35]

Finally, it has to be pointed out again that the standard of human containment within our prisons in many instances remains diabolical. Is it any wonder so many inmates are hardened and more embittered when they emerge? Is it any wonder so many take drugs while they are inside to beat the pain and boredom? Is it any wonder serious crime is escalating on the outside when we are producing such an array of hardened graduates from the inside?

We need to remind ourselves in all our dealings with the criminal justice system of the need to protect human dignity. If we fail in this, then we return to practising little less than a form of barbarism. Until our society grapples adequately with the shortcomings of a retributive criminal justice philosophy, we will continue to have increasing crime rates, higher imprisonment numbers, less safety in the community, and an extremely expensive ever-expanding prison system.

Footnotes

1. *New Zealand Herald*, 14 May 1993
2. *New Zealand Herald*, 26 February 1994
3. *New Zealand Herald*, 26 February 1994
4. Resource Implications of the Report of the Ministerial Inquiry into the Prison System 1989, Justice Department, October 1989
5. Department of Statistics reports 1983, 1993
6. *New Zealand Herald*, 26 February 1994
7. Hon. Douglas Graham, speech, 22 February 1991
8. UUSC National Moratorium on Prison Construction, Boston, Massachusetts
9. Justice Department report, December 1993
10. *The Press*, Christchurch, 30 December 1993
11. Penal Policy Review, Government Print, 1981
12. Justice Department report, September 1988
13. *Financial Times*, London, January 1993
14. Tony Short, *Whatever Happened to the Fair Go? New Zealand in the 1990s*, University of South Australia, 1993
15. *The Press*, Christchurch, 30 December 1992
16. *Christchurch Mail*, 30 August 1993
17. Phillip Berrigan, *Widen the Prison Gates*, Simon and Schuster, New York, 1973
18. *The Press*, Christchurch, 23 July 1993
19. *Auckland Star*, 11 February 1991. Full report presented at a public meeting in Auckland on prison violence, 15 February 1991
20. *The Press*, Christchurch, 27 January 1994
21. *Greymouth Evening Star*, 5 April 1988
22. Debbie Martin, paper presented at seminar 'Home Grown '93', 25 November 1993
23. *The Press*, Christchurch, 27 January 1994
24. *The Press*, Christchurch, 30 August 1994
25. Mike Martin, *NZ Listener*, 22 June 1985
26. *The Press*, Christchurch, 30 December 1993
27. *The Press*, Christchurch, 24 September 1993
28. Julie Liebrich, *Straight to the Point – Angles on Giving Up Crime*, Otago University Press, Dunedin, September 1993
29. *Sunday Times*, 9 February 1992
30. Julie Liebrich, op cit
31. Report, 'A Time for Justice', British Catholic Social Welfare Commission, 1982
32. M. H. Bremner, *Mental Illness and the Economy*, Harvard University, 1973
33. Jim Consedine, *A Poison in the Bloodstream*, Cape Catley, Picton, September 1990
34. Hon. Douglas Graham, speech, 22 February 1991
35. Peter Williams Q.C., speech, Criminal Bar Association, Auckland, 26 May 1989

CHAPTER THREE

Advance Australia Unfair

Australian society seems to be less punitive than either the United States or New Zealand. The reasons are probably many and varied. White Australia's origins as a convict settlement may play some part in the formation of the Australian psyche, resulting in this less punitive attitude. Whatever the reasons, Australia imprisons at about two-thirds the rate of New Zealand and one-sixth that of the US.

Despite its positive relativity, Australia still has a high imprisonment rate. It follows the patterns of all democratic countries by imprisoning the poor, the vulnerable, the dispossessed and, of course, its Aborigines, in totally disproportionate numbers.

As a major report on Australian prisons pointed out, prison still exists as a powerful emotional and symbolic answer to the crisis of control that exists in society, a guarantee of the state's ability to exercise law and order.[1]

Background

Social conditions in Australia, as in all socially developed countries, have deteriorated markedly as the effect of monetarist economic policies bites into the economic wellbeing of the lower income groupings. As usual the most severely hit are the poor and the vulnerable, the elderly without substantial assets, single-parent families, the sick, the mentally ill, the young (especially those poorly skilled), the indigenous population, and immigrants. As in all similar societies, it is from these groupings that the prison population is primarily drawn.

Poverty is on the increase. An often-quoted set of conclusions published by Professor John Piggott in 1984 is that the wealthiest 1 percent of adults individually hold 25 percent of private wealth, the top 5 percent hold about 50 percent and the top 10 percent hold about 60 percent.[2]

A.W. Dilnot estimated that the least wealthy 30 percent hold no net wealth at all and have more liabilities than assets.[3] The top 1 percent were earning an amount equal to the bottom 21 percent.[4] In June 1992, 35.8 percent of young people were unemployed in a nation with an 11.1 percent unemployment rate.[5]

Child poverty has increased dramatically in Australia since the late 1970s as a result of unemployment, housing costs and marriage breakdowns.[6] There are now approximately 700,000 children living in poverty in Australia, with a further 500 children being added to the total every day.[7] According to a study carried out at Macquarie University in Sydney, 25 percent of Australia's schoolchildren live in poverty.

There were at least 25,000 children homeless in 1989, according to the Burdenkin Report. By 1991 Commissioner Burdenkin's estimate had risen to 50,000. In just two years the number had doubled. Other estimates double or treble that figure. In New South Wales alone, a youth accommodation survey in June 1991 showed there to be up to 30,000 homeless youths.

Poverty of this magnitude inevitably leaves its imprint on other sectors of society. According to an Institute of Criminology report in January 1993, of all the people taken into custody in the previous year, a phenomenal 52.1 percent were there for fines default. This was more than double that of five years earlier.[8] This figure draws a very clear link between poverty and imprisonment. It is of interest to note that New Zealand has, by way of legislation in 1993, virtually abolished imprisonment for fines default.

Poverty is worst among Aborigines. According to the Catholic Aboriginal and Islander Council of Queensland, 48 percent of Aborigines live below the poverty line. Their general rate of unemployment is four times that of others. Their life expectancy is about 20 years less than that of the general population.

Twenty years ago, 100 in every 1000 Aboriginal babies died before their first birthday. In April 1994 *Time* magazine reported that the situation remained unchanged.

Similarly, it reported that in 1971, a survey at Royal Darwin Hospital showed that one in five Top End Aboriginal children suffered malnutrition before their second birthday. A 1993 study found no change. In some Aboriginal communities, half the children suffer malnutrition. This is a worse rate than in Kurdish or Somali refugee camps.

The report went on to say that more than 30 percent of Aboriginal people are homeless or inadequately housed. Almost all Aboriginal babies have ear infections within the first month of life and few receive treatment, meaning that up to half of them will have some hearing loss. Deafness means problems at school, if there is a school, and if the child attends. Nationally, a quarter of Aboriginal children leave school before the end of their 10th year.

The 'feminisation of poverty' is an expression that has now entered the nation's vocabulary. This reflects the fact that after children, it is women who suffer most from the effects of poverty. Up to 50 percent of sole-parent families headed by women live in poverty.[9]

Profile

That rising poverty levels lead to more crime is obvious. The more structured the economic gap between those with wealth and those without, the more the prison numbers have reflected this basic inequality of opportunity. There are other factors involved in rising crime rates – unemployment, the break-up of family life, and the widespread addiction to drugs being three.

The Australian Institute of Criminology in February 1988 provided this profile of a typical prisoner:

> The prisoner is likely to be a male between 20 and 29 years, Australian-born, in certain states and prisons Aboriginal, a person who has not completed a secondary education, unemployed at the time of the offence.
>
> A relatively large number of persons appearing before the courts suffer some sort of intellectual disability. About 10 percent of the Australian prison population are intellectually handicapped, and a substantial number are psychologically disturbed. A high percentage of prisoners are affected by alcohol at the time of their offending.[10]

Australia has six state and two territory penal systems and a federal national one. As in the United States, often the rate of incarceration varies from state to state. In 1991, the rate of imprisonment was 69 per 100,000 population in Queensland, 100 in New South Wales, 51 in Victoria, 114 in Western Australia, and the national average was 81 per 100,000. Yet there is little if any variation in crime rates in these four states. Simply, some states imprison at higher rates than others. For example, New South Wales has twice as many prisoners as Victoria, yet they share an identical crime rate.[11]

Commenting on such figures, the former director of the Australian Institute of Criminology, William Clifford, said research showed that there was no relationship between levels of crime and rates of imprisonment.[12]

As in most countries, the view presented by the media and often by politicians is that prisons are full of people who are a risk to the community. The fact that nearly 60 percent of prisoners in Australia are non-violent offenders is ignored, as indeed is the reality that most of those convicted of violence are not a threat either. Repeat violent offenders are a small minority of those convicted.

Prison Life

In 1989 the Combined Australian Churches produced a report containing a savage indictment of prison conditions in Australia. In *Prison, the Last Resort*, they described the process of being imprisoned in the infamous Pentridge Jail in Sydney.

They wrote that as soon as prisoners arrive in Pentridge they are herded in like animals and stripped naked in front of strangers. They are then put into yards until they are classified (according to their crime). They may spend up to eight weeks in the yard before being classified. If they are not convicted and refused bail, they can wait up to 18 months or more.

The yards are filthy, with cold concrete seats, and the toilets have no doors. They are there winter and summer under all conditions. This is disputed on the basis that they are under cover, but cover consists of a roof, like a carport, which is open in the front. After the yards they are classified to a country jail or to Pentridge.

This description by an unnamed Pentridge inmate says it all:

> If you have a job you are lucky. If not, you are put in a wired compound, to walk up and down all day. Even a prisoner can cope with this to a degree, but what the public is not told is how the governors can make life hard, via the prison officers, if you have a fall-out with the governor or the officers.[13]

Australian prisons in general are just as tough as their American and New Zealand counterparts. Government personnel confirm the harshness of the treatment. A medical officer writes:

> Prisoners get degrading and dictatorial treatment from many prison officers ... I have seen the results of the systematic beating of large numbers of prisoners as retribution – no charges are laid. Moreover, prisoners can be denied access to medical treatment at the whim of prison officers.[14]

A prison officer speaks in the report of the frequent tension and sometimes fear where standover tactics and assaults by prisoners on prisoners are the norm.[15]

A Catholic sister involved in prison work writes of the effect of the prison environment on the life and spirit of an inmate:

> First, imagine a world without nature, animals, little children, the opposite sex and elderly couples. Imagine a world where you have literally no choice day after day. Your clothes, food, timetable, contact with your family, leisure and work are determined in most cases for you. Your personal environment is a mix of companions you did not choose: first offenders with lifers, property offenders with offenders against the person – a mix that has led prison to be described as 'a university of crime'.
>
> Imagine being locked away in your room from 4.15pm until 7.30am – often a shared room. Think for a moment what such a combination could mean for personal development, for the establishment of a healthy human relationship, for a wholesome creative relationship with nature. It is a recipe for personal destruction. It is a destructiveness which reaches out even to the innocent families of offenders, a destructiveness which extends even to those who work within the system.[16]

Jailspeak is as prevalent in Australia as it is anywhere. In the past four years the NSW government has talked of rehabilitation in prisons. At the same time it has encouraged an increase of more than 50 percent in the state's prison population, caused the gravest overcrowding in living memory, reduced expenditure on prison education and welfare services, failed to create work opportunities to keep pace with the expanding prison population, reduced support for prisoner families and support groups, built new prisons in remote places distant from the residential communities from which the inmates come, and removed from prison cells such items as religious ornaments and study books.[17]

NSW politicians have 'talked up' the law and order hype in recent years, resulting in the state leaping ahead of other similar-sized states such as Victoria in terms of numbers in jail. In a mere four years, 1990-94, the prison population increased by an extraordinary 60 percent, with the state government either building or planning to build five new prisons costing hundreds of millions of dollars. All this to meet the results of their own eloquence!

Further, the so-called 'truth in sentencing' law of 1989 means that prisoners have to spend three-quarters of their sentence in jail instead of about one-third, with no room for remission for good behaviour and allowing for much less time for supervised parole in the community.

A report issued by the police in November 1994 showed that while crime figures in most categories had dropped in NSW, fear levels were growing among citizens. It showed that 58 percent feared being attacked, 48 percent feared being murdered, and 25 percent feared their children might be abused or sexually assaulted. The key reason given for this high level of community apprehension was the hype of politicians and the media. It had nothing to do with the reality of crime levels.

Sydney lawyer Jim Coombs, who has worked with inmates at Long Bay Prison, says the community should be very clear about the nature of prisons in Australia. He describes them as degrading, dehumanising, deskilling and depressing. He says Australian jails are terrible, with bashings and homosexual rapes occurring daily, and forcible injection of hard drugs with used (and quite possibly Aids-contaminated) needles quite common. The time spent in jail by prisoners is wasted time, or, worse, time spent in the process of being corrupted.

One of the most offensive things about our jails is the waste of human life and ability that they represent. Prisoners can spend 16 hours a day locked in a cell, the remaining eight walking up and down the yards. Hardly a life for a person who will need all the resources he can muster to survive without crime when released. The most feeble attempts have been made to put prisoners to work. These days there are almost no prison industries.

The experience that stands starkly in Coomb's memory is of an inspection made early in the 1980s of the part of Long Bay used for holding prisoners who were clearly deranged, known as an OBS (standing for observation) cell. It was a filthy cage, with faeces smeared on the walls. The prisoners there were doped to incoherence with largactil, some almost catatonic. A couple of tense and bored prison officers watched to arrest any outbreak of violence, and a nurse administered the drug. That part of the jail has closed, but the lack of adequate psychiatric services continues.[18]

Prison life also leads to a high rate of suicide. A study published in 1990 by the Australian and New Zealand Association of Psychiatry found that 'prolonged imprisonment and dehumanising conditions' in New South Wales prisons were major contributors to the increase in suicides in custody. The study found that the New South Wales correctional conditions, policies and practices fell far behind the standards and principles adopted as minimum standards by the United Nations in 1980.

A 1990 newspaper report revealed that in NSW the suicide rate among prisoners had grown from an average 90 per 100,000 prisoners in 1973-84 to 200 per 100,000 in the late 1980s – 17 times higher than the rate for the general population. The report examined 129 suicides in NSW prisons between 1980 and 1984 and found that 64 percent committed suicide within the first six months in custody, while 47 percent were awaiting trial.[19]

Prison life has its own unofficial hierarchy and economic system. The problem of drugs in prison needs to be seen in the context of these unofficial structures. Often drugs and the payments used for them form the economic backbone of the black market within the prison. Assaults and beatings are a not uncommon result of dealing to a non-paying debtor. Theft from other inmates is another way of meeting drug debts for the desperate. All such activities form part of the prison culture.

Because inmates are totally shut off from the outside world, they become part of a community, with its own values, language and ways. This is why 'narking' is regarded as such a heinous sin among inmates. It breaks down the tight prisoner community, allowing outside agents to become involved.

The code of prison conduct demands that officers be kept at a certain distance and treated with suspicion and a certain amount of contempt. They are never to be trusted. It also works the other way: prisoners are always treated with some degree of suspicion by officers. Never let your guard down, is a common approach with prison officers.

This negative culture is the principal reason that therapeutic programmes will only ever have very limited success within the traditional environment. Negativity breeds cynicism and mistrust. No matter how well a programme may be conducted within the prison during working hours, the 18 hours spent in the wings and cells after each session undo most of the good done. Prisons cannot rehabilitate and punish at the same time.

Women in Prison

In the past 10 years the number of women in Australian prisons has more than doubled. This is partly as a result of sentencing policy but mainly as a result of the upsurge in drug-related offending. This type of offending is greater in percentage terms among women than men. In 1988 approximately 80 percent of female crime was drug-related.

Like the men, the majority of women in prison are young and poor. They are not well educated, most of them having had less than three years of secondary education. Over three-quarters are in low-paid jobs or unemployed, fewer than half are married or in de facto relationships. Most are convicted of drug-related crimes, welfare fraud and spouse homicide, in that order. As the Churches' report found, there was some evidence that women also suffer from discriminatory sentencing in regard to prostitution (where prostitutes but few clients are jailed) and spouse homicide (where they receive harsher sentences than men – even where the women have been subject to years of violence). Women are more likely to be imprisoned for first offences and less likely to be included in programmes that are an alternative to prison.[20]

Aborigines in Prison

Far and away the most appalling dimension of the Australian prison system is the number of Aboriginal people there. In 1982, when they constituted less than 2 percent of the population, they accounted for 30 percent of all those in prison.[21]

It is only since 1981 that separate figures have been kept for Aboriginal prison rates. Nationally, Aboriginal people are now incarcerated in police custody at 29 times the rate to that of the general population, and in prison custody at 17 times that rate.[22]

In 1991, Sir Ronald Wilson, president of the Human Rights and Equal Opportunities Commission, spoke to a seminar about the position of Aborigines in the criminal justice system and the reasons they make up such disproportionate numbers. He said that the most significant factor contributing to the over-representation of Aboriginal people in custody continues to be the disadvantaged and unequal position to which they are relegated socially, culturally and economically.

Poverty, inadequate living conditions and consequent poor health are just some factors that reduce the ability of Aboriginal people to assert their autonomy and take control of their lives. Added to that is the lingering legacy of inequities in education and employment, which continues to hinder the efforts of the people themselves.

It is hard to argue against the proposition that it is rough justice that an Aboriginal person in Western Australia is 43 times more likely to be taken into police custody than a non-Aboriginal. Aborigines make up less than 3 percent of the state's population, yet account for 51 percent of all people sentenced by High Courts to imprisonment. However, 75 percent are there for less than three months – in other words, 75 percent of Aboriginal prisoners probably do not need to be incarcerated.[23]

As the Churches' report observed, part of the reason for the high imprisonment rate has been the discriminatory laws aimed at Aborigines. They charged that since the beginning of European occupation, Aboriginal people have been denied the vote, disqualified from various forms of social security, denied the right to buy liquor, discriminated against in labour laws, had their children taken away without real cause, and been subjected to the whims of so-called protection laws.

Myths have been developed to justify this discrimination. Aboriginal people are described as being lesser people than whites, more troublesome, and more in need of control and punishment. These myths have contributed to difficult relationships between Aboriginal people and the police and courts. Aboriginal people find themselves discriminated against at every step of the legal process: in the chances of being charged, in the difficulty of getting legal assistance and bail, and in the severity of the sentence passed.[24]

Aborigines also die in prison in disproportionate numbers. This subject is dealt with more fully in the chapter on Aboriginal justice. Between 1980 and 1987, 106 Aborigines died in police or prison custody in Australia. The head of the Royal Commission into Aboriginal Deaths in Custody, Mr Justice Muirhead, has pointed out that if white Australians had died at the same rate, 7400 would have died during the same period.[25]

Conclusion

The obvious conclusion one must draw from this brief outline is that the retributive justice system in Australia does not serve its citizens well. At $A50,000 per head[26] they are being badly short-changed in their penal policy. Australia imprisons Aborigines at a scandalous level. Their philosophy of retribution has brought nothing but mayhem and widespread distress to families caught up in it, and death and disaster to Aborigines. It has guaranteed a growing level of crime and wasted billions of dollars of taxpayers' money.

Footnotes

1. *Prison, the Last Resort*, report of the Combined Australian Churches, 1989, p8
2. *Common Wealth for the Common Good*, Australian Catholic Bishops Conference, Collins Dove, Victoria, 1992, p49
3. *Australian Economic Review*, 1st Quarter, 1990
4. 'Income Distribution in Australia', 1983-89, Research Paper No 340
5. *Common Wealth*, op cit, p 60

6. Ibid p 72

7. *The Age*, Melbourne, 29 May 1992

8. *The Bulletin*, 18 January 1994

9. *Common Wealth*, op cit, p77

10. *Prison, the Last Resort*, op cit, p11

11. Ian Hill, *Prison the Last Option*, conference paper, 18 October 1991, Perth, Western Australia. Published by the Anglican, Catholic and Uniting Churches of Australia, Perth, p16

12. *Auckland Star*, 4 November 1982

13. *Prison, the Last Resort*, op cit, p21

14. Ibid

15. Ibid

16. Ibid

17. Tony Vinson, Allan Nixon Memorial Lecture, Auckland, 3 September 1992

18. *National Outlook*, September 1988, p11

19. *Otago Daily Times*, 6 November 1990

20. *Prison, the Last Resort*, op cit, p 13

21. *Auckland Star*, 4 November 1982

22. *Western Australian*, 21 June 1988

23. Ronald Wilson, *Prison the Last Option*, conference paper, 18 October 1991, Perth, Western Australia. Published by the Anglican, Catholic and Uniting Churches of Australia, Perth, p4

24. *Prison, the Last Resort*, op cit, p13

25. Final report, Royal Commission of Inquiry into Aboriginal Deaths in Custody, 1991

26. *The Bulletin*, 11 January 1994

CHAPTER FOUR

Retribution: the British Way

Prison is an expensive way of making bad people worse.

Government White Paper, House of Commons, 1990

Ripon is a small northern Yorkshire town of 12,000, sited on the Ure River. As long ago as the year 934, King Athelstan granted the church there the right to offer sanctuary. This meant that law-breakers could not be prosecuted within certain boundaries but instead, after seeking sanctuary, were handed over to the canons of the cathedral. From them they could usually hope to receive just and humane treatment.

Ripon also has one of the earliest prisons in England, euphemistically called 'the House of Correction'. It was built in 1686 alongside an already existing debtors' prison. In England the poor have always had to pay their dues. In 1815 it was decided to add a prison block and to lock up wrongdoers other than vagrants, with separate wings for men and women.

The treadmill was used extensively in Ripon from 1820 to 1866, and the stocks were last used in 1859 for a man found drunk in Allhallowgate. Treadmilling was gruelling and unproductive. Up to 10,000 treads a day were made by prisoners going nowhere. Ten prisoners at a time could be 'corrected' on this diabolical machine.

To visit the Ripon Prison and Police Museum is to recall the history of punishment in Britain in the past 1000 years. It is also to come up against a cold hard fact: the philosophy of Ripon's early days is still the driving force behind British criminal justice today. Ripon's philosophy of 1686, a mixed cocktail of 'correction' and punishment tempered by a dash of incentive and reform, is the same philosophy that produced the amendments to the Criminal Justice Act in 1993.

Yet it need not have been so. The Strangeways riot in Manchester in April 1990, following so soon on the riots in Hull, the Isle of Wight and Gloucester, and the burning of Northeye, should have produced a turning point for the British penal system. The riot could have been a catalyst, or even an excuse, for long-overdue reforms to the philosophy of retribution that has dominated the monstrous history of penal sanction in Britain.

Britain has practised them all – from a massive array of executions in the 19th century (over 200 offences attracted the death penalty), through transportation first to the United States and then to Australia, then the period of the 'hulk' ships off the coast, followed by the draconian days of Victorian prisons with their floggings, hard labour and spartan living conditions, to the modern, soul-destroying, electronically controlled maximum- and medium-security institutions. All follow the same retributive philosophy – punish and avenge. All use the same dehumanising techniques – isolation, boredom, dependency, coercion.

Strangeways came at a time when penal reform was already on the front pages. The riot brought nightly scenes of chaos and disorder into the lounges of the nation via television as the men on the roof clung to their defiance.

Just how far modern Britain has moved from any semblance of a just and fair society was reflected in those distant rooftop figures. For 25 days they waved from the rooftops, trying to communicate to the wider public their despair, their anger, their hopelessness, while police sirens wailed every time they tried to speak. Mostly unemployed, mostly addicts of one form or another, mostly homeless, many psychiatrically disturbed, they represented a class of people structured out of mainstream life in Britain. They had nothing to lose by their action.

As prison chaplain Willie Slavin says, prisons increasingly have acted as a backstop for the social services.

> Prisons have become a 'third world' in our midst. Here is the flotsam and jetsam of our society, the redundant and the rejected. They suffer massively from alcoholism, and increasingly from drug addiction. Often they have been involved in the black economy, or in petty crime such as stealing vehicles. Clearly missing are those who mainly benefit from crime: the financiers who launder ill-gotten gains, well-heeled gangsters, tax evaders, cowboy operators, police who are perjurers, abusers of women ... Almost all come from the marginalised sections of the community.[1]

A caring government should have been able to look beyond the immediate problems caused by the riot and listen to the governor of the prison, Brendan O'Friel, when he made his plea for a more humane system of justice. He spoke of 'an explosion of evil' that occurred when the pent-up emotions of the inmates were unleashed in an orgy of violence and revenge. He believes that official policy towards inmates is still clouded by the 'hulks' mentality of the 19th century, when hulks moored off the coast kept prisoners out of sight, out of mind.

The situation had been brought about by a whole range of interconnected social polices that needed to be addressed. Inside the prison, the situation of long remands, protection prisoners, overcrowding (up to three in a cell built for one), lack of education facilities and programmes, and the plight of mentally disturbed inmates all cried out for immediate attention. The outside needs of more jobs, better housing, drugs in the community, the spiritual malaise, poverty, poor parenting skills, racial issues, were all apparent to community workers and local leaders. What was clearly needed was a widespread policy of change.

It was not to be. Instead, Strangeways came and went and it was business as usual for the authorities. Until the next time. And the next. And the next, when the same explosive cocktail of causes will ignite into another riot, in another place, over the same issues.

How did the criminal justice system get so bad that thousands get locked away in little concrete rooms for years on end? What pressures lead them eventually to revolt as they did at Strangeways? How did this violent and degrading retributive system ever get a grip on Britain and later her colonies?

The criminal justice history of most cultures – Polynesian, African, Celtic to name but three – has been entirely different. According to the Jubilee Policy Group's report in December 1992, ancient cultures viewed crime essentially as a personal event. Although it breached the common welfare, the offence was still seen principally as a violation against the victim, and the offender was held responsible to settle that account with the victim.

To avoid an endless cycle of vengeance and violence, legal codes, issued between 2050BC and AD600 in places as far afield as Babylon, Rome and Kent concentrated on restitution as a means to wipe out the consequences of the offender's actions on the victim, to make up for the losses and to help restore community peace and order. The modern view of the state monopoly on justice arose to protect individuals from the uncontrollable violence of blood feuds. Private vengeance was taken over by the community to ensure it was limited to reasonable proportions. Restitution was not an end in itself. The commitment required by the criminal justice system was not only to address the wrong, but also to vindicate the victim, reconcile the parties, and re-establish community peace.[2]

The Jubilee Policy document goes on to explain how community-based justice gave way to a state-controlled process in Britain. It says that until the rise of the European nation states and the consolidation of the institution of the monarchy, the victim was always the central focus.

Some writers have pinpointed the paradigm shift away from this at the time of the Norman invasion. William the Conqueror and his descendants had to struggle with the barons and other authorities for political power. They found the legal process a highly effective instrument in asserting their dominance over secular matters and, through their control of the courts, in increasing their political authority.

To this end, William's son, Henry I, issued in 1116 the *Leges Henrici*, creating the idea of the 'King's Peace' and asserting royal jurisdiction over certain offences by which it was deemed to have been violated. These included arson, robbery, murder, false coinage and crimes of violence. A violation of the King's Peace was a violation against his person, and thus the King became the primary victim in such offences, taking the place of the victim before the law. The actual victim lost his position in the process and the state and the offender were left as the sole concerned parties.

As a result the system, rather than being concerned to make the victim whole, now focused on upholding the authority of the state. It centred on the offender, rather than the victim, since it was concerned with why the law had been broken, and how to stop it being broken again. Criminal justice became future-orientated, concerned rather to make the offender and potential offenders law-abiding, than to make them atone for their past offence. Restitution, being past-orientated and concerned with the victim, was gradually abandoned. Monies which would have been paid to the victim were now paid to the state, and thus took on a punitive rather than a compensatory role, becoming what we know as a fine. Many cruel and humiliating forms of corporal punishment were also used.[3]

Crime in Britain

Despite nearly 1000 years of punishment-orientated retributive justice, crime in Britain is endemic. Something is not working. However, about three-quarters of it is not recorded in the official figures.

The Home Office conducts annual surveys called the British Crime Survey. This does not consider offences already notified. It is based on interviews with one person over 16 years of age in each of 11,000 households. The results of this survey show that there are about 21 million crimes a year, four times the official figure. Many of these offences are of a very minor type that would be most unlikely to result in any form of sanction. Scotland has its own independent criminal justice system.

In 1988 the police in England and Wales recorded 3.7 million notifiable offences against property. In 80 percent of reported thefts, the value of the goods stolen was under £500, and in half of the cases less than £100. Violent crimes against the person, sexual offences and robbery amounted to 5.1 percent. Dealing with crime in England and Wales is expensive. The annual expenditure on the criminal justice system is £7 billion (about $NZ20 billion), an increase of 77 percent in the past 10 years.[4]

By 1991 the number of notified crimes had risen to 5.3 million. Ninety percent of those were crimes against property; one-third of these involved either stealing cars or having goods stolen from them. One-quarter involved burglary. Another 18 percent involved criminal damage and 6 percent were violent crime, including sexual offences.

Vivien Stern, director of NACRO, the National Association for the Care and Resettlement of Offenders, provides some interesting data. Of every 100 offences committed, 41 are reported to the police. The police analyse and sift the information they have been given, reducing the number to 26. They are successful in laying a charge in seven of these cases, and then the criminal justice process starts. There is an outcome in four of the seven offences: one offender will admit guilt and be cautioned, three will be convicted.[5]

In other words, far more people commit crime than ever come to the notice of the police. It confirms what criminologist Allan Nixon always said about the them-and-us attitude that most people have towards offenders. He used to say that most people were prone to law-breaking when it suited them, but that only a few ever got caught up in the criminal justice system.

This may be for a variety of reasons, among them the fact that serious crimes committed by 'blue-collar' offenders will be more severely policed than either 'white-collar' crimes or minor ones.

Education, race, class and location largely determine whether a person ends up in the criminal justice system. A recent survey showed 15 percent of prisoners had a reading age of 10 years or less, and 30 percent had played truant at school. Over 80 percent of prison inmates have no school qualification. Several recent reports have also accused various police forces in England and Wales of racism in their approach to their duties. Special programmes are now run in some forces to help police recognise their own basic racist tendencies.

Racism is not confined to policing. There are structural problems elsewhere. Sir Sonny Ramphal, former Secretary-general of the Commonwealth, in a lecture to the British Bar Council in 1990, said:

> Speaking of Britain, the legal system has attracted considerable public criticism both as regards the profession and also the way the courts treat the black population ... The concept of 'equality before the law' can be an extraordinarily difficult one to realise in a multicultural society where law is, inevitably, and for reasons of history, in the hands of a single dominant culture.

Britain has always been a class-ridden society and this is reflected in the prison statistics, especially in relation to the unemployed. Even more striking is the relationship between unemployment and imprisonment. Researchers who had analysed trends in crime and unemployment rates since the war calculated that, after allowing for any increase in crime, for every 1000 people unemployed in England and Wales, there were 14 more receptions into prison. For every 1000 more young people unemployed, an extra 56 young people were jailed.[6]

The National Prison Survey found that 33 percent of prisoners had been unemployed, compared to 10 percent of the general population. Another survey found that 64 percent of young offenders were unemployed when arrested. The same survey found that 20 percent of prisoners were mentally disturbed, and three percent had 'mental disorders of the kind which would justify compulsory detention in hospital for treatment'.[7]

Homelessness is a major problem for prisoners. Adrian Speller of the British Council of Churches Penal Policy Group says in his book *Breaking Out* that it has been estimated that as many as 58 percent of those released from prison in London and the southeast may be without a home to which they can return. In other parts of the country it is between one-third and one-quarter. Without a base in the community, the chances of successful resettlement are slim. Without an address, it is difficult for ex-prisoners to claim social security benefits. Without reasonable accommodation, it is extremely difficult to obtain work. There is evidence from Home Office studies that accommodation obtained by homeless ex-prisoners is usually at a lower level than that which they had before imprisonment.[8]

Only half the prisoners released in 1991 said they would be going back to their previous accommodation. A quarter of young people remanded in custody expected to be homeless on release, joining the estimated 135,000 young people in Britain without a home. In a survey of homeless people, 35 percent said they had spent some time in custody.[9] Before they came to prison, 83 percent had somewhere relatively settled to live. Only seven percent lived in hostels or on the streets. By the time they had to leave prison, half of those who had somewhere to live had lost their homes.[10]

Home Office research shows that, as in other similar countries, re-offending rates for ex-prison inmates in Britain are extremely high. Among teenagers, a whopping 92 percent re-offend within a two-year period. In other words, only eight juveniles out of every 100 'go straight' upon release. For youths under 21, the reconviction rate is 71 percent within two years and 82 percent within four. For adult males, 57 percent re-offend within two years and 68 percent within four. And for adult women, the re-offending rate is 40 percent within two years and 48 percent within four.[11]

Fast Forward

Britain has always imprisoned in disproportionate numbers the downtrodden, rejected, homeless, dispossessed and victims of prejudice and economic injustice. As Vivien Stern of NACRO said in delivering the Allan Nixon Memorial Lecture:

> Our prison system is a monstrous leftover from an earlier age. When you walk into one of our old Victorian prisons you feel you are stepping back into another

century – the bare grey walls, the little dungeon-like windows, the prison officers in uniforms signifying a bygone notion of authority, the gruesome humiliating rituals, such as slopping out.[9]

Sadly, things have taken a turn for the worse. What had seemed like the light at the end of a long tunnel has been extinguished. The late 1980s had brought a surge of hope to compassionate people involved in prison work: it seemed that at long last Britain would adopt a more modern humane attitude towards offenders and its prison system. This had followed on a reduction in criminal offending in 1988-89, and a realisation within government circles that the cries from the trenches were genuine and needed attention.

Douglas Hurd had replaced Leon Brittan as Home Secretary in late 1983 and had taken his duties seriously. A light was dawning on the wider echelons of Conservative Party policy-makers and the government that things had to change. Under Hurd at the Home Office a new strategy developed. Its first component was in the way crime was presented. It was to be always placed in context.

For example, to counter the tabloid mentality that everyone should be cowering in their homes because of the murderers, rapists and muggers on the loose, the British Crime Survey came up with a statistic that an adult in Britain could expect to experience a robbery once every five centuries, an injurious assault once every century, for the family car to be stolen once in every 60 years, and could expect to be burgled once in every 40 years.

The message went out, proven from the statistical information, that levels of crime were not related to levels of imprisonment. Nor were they related to the severity of punishment from the courts. They were related to whether people locked their homes and cars, kept a dog, whether local authorities put up good lighting and had adequate public transport from the city to the suburbs for the drinkers at the end of the night's revelry.

More deeply, it was suggested they were related to social factors – for example, how people brought up their children, the level of discipline or lack of it in the home or school, the working of the labour market, levels of affluence and housing conditions. Indeed the Home Office actually commissioned research that set out 'to explore the range of factors, particularly economic factors, believed to be related to crime'.[13]

The study concluded that economic factors have a major influence on trends in both property and personal crime. It appeared that:

> … in the years when people are increasing their spending little, or even reducing it, property crime tends to grow relatively quickly. Whereas in years when people are rapidly increasing their expenditure, property crime tends to grow less rapidly or even fall.[14]

The government Green Paper 'Punishment, Custody and the Community', published in July 1988, was followed by a supplementary paper, 'Tackling Offending: An Action Plan'. This led to a White Paper, 'Crime, Justice and Protecting the Public' being presented to the House of Commons in February 1990, calling for wide-ranging reforms in how criminal justice was to be serviced.

In many ways the White Paper was conservative. It adopted the sour-sweet approach, maintaining a clear focus on punishment. It held to the retributive philosophy that 'punishment has a major part to play in reducing crime, but its role must not be overstated'. It also concluded that 'long prison sentences are the right punishment for certain types of serious offence'. Long-term prisoners were to be kept in longer. Crimes of violence were to be punished more harshly. The paper made it clear that the government's aim was to punish, and that criminals should get their 'just desserts'.[15]

> Punishment can effectively denounce criminal behaviour and exact retribution for it. The sentence of the court expresses public repugnance of criminal behaviour and determines the punishment for it.[16]

At the same time it was a reform paper, providing a shift in emphasis. It recognised that prisons no longer provided realistic rehabilitation. A shift in philosophy was needed. The paper said it was once believed that prison, properly used, could encourage a high proportion of offenders to start an honest life on their release. Nobody now regards imprisonment, in itself, as an effective means of reform for most prisoners. No matter how hard prison staff try to inject a positive purpose, prison remains a society that requires virtually no sense of personal responsibility from inmates. Normal social or working habits do not fit.

The opportunity to learn from other criminals is pervasive, the paper found. For most offenders, imprisonment has to be justified in terms of public protection, denunciation and retribution. Otherwise it can be an expensive way of making bad people worse.[17]

The White Paper encouraged compensation to victims, developed a system for unit fines, promoted community-based options to imprisonment 'as being better for the victim, the public and the offender than a custodial sentence'. It gave the courts new powers to combine penalties such as compensation, supervision and fines. It promoted community service orders and probation as alternatives to imprisonment. It demanded that before it gave a custodial sentence, a court had to be satisfied that the offence be so serious that a custodial sentence was justified, and necessary to protect the public from serious harm. The court should also give reasons for its decision.[18]

The paper also recognised the limitations of deterrence, describing it as a principle with immediate appeal. Most law-abiding citizens understand the reasons why some behaviour is made a criminal offence, and would be deterred by the shame of a conviction or the possibility of a severe penalty. There are doubtless some criminals who carefully calculate the possible gains and risks.

But much crime is committed on impulse, given the opportunity being presented by an open window or an unlocked door, and it is committed by offenders who live from moment to moment. Their crimes are as impulsive as the rest of their reckless, sad or pathetic lives. It is unrealistic to construct sentencing arrangements on the assumption that most offenders will weigh up the possibilities in advance and base their conduct on rational calculation. Often they do not.[19]

It also provided for a marvellous new unit payment system of fines. This was to overcome the obvious injustice under the prevailing system whereby the courts took little account of the income of the offender. People were fined according to the offence, regardless of their income. This was particularly obvious with automatic fines. The net result might be that two people, one a millionaire and the other a beneficiary, would be convicted of the same offence and fined equal amounts. For the millionaire it would be no punishment at all. For the beneficiary it might mean a period without food or an inability to pay a power account or the rent.

The principle of the unit fines system was that an offender paid a certain percentage of disposable income per week. An offence might be serious enough to be judged to be worth a fine of 10 units. An offender with a disposable income after meeting all basic needs of $20 a week would pay $200 as the fine. Another poorer person with only $5 disposable per week would pay $50. The philosophy underpinning this approach is based on fairness and economic position before the law, and the principle that rich and poor should be treated equally by the law, but not necessarily treated the same. Such a philosophy is of the essence of true justice.

In 1988, 16,800 people had been imprisoned for fines default: 3 percent of the prison population. Most simply could not afford to pay. This results in a grave injustice and stigma for the defaulters, their families, and the taxpayer, who had to pay up to £300 a week per capita for each one imprisoned.

After considerable community and parliamentary debate, legislation was enacted in 1991 in the Criminal Justice Act. The next four months saw 4000 fewer in prison, a marked rise in community service orders, and a lessening of probation and suspended sentences.

Return to Square One

This brief respite in a 1000-year history of retributive punitive action was not to last. The right wing of the governing Conservative Party cried foul when they saw their position of privilege before the law being eroded. Several highly publicised cases of recently released offenders committing crimes and some obviously absurd abnormalities in the unit fines system combined to form the base from which a backlash resulted.

A well-constructed and directed media campaign sought to have the old regime reimposed, with heavy prison sentences as its central platform. Alongside this came a series of strident speeches from successive new Home Secretaries, Kenneth Clarke and Michael Howard, advocating a greater use of imprisonment. This led to the 1991 act being considerably weakened in 1993 by amendments including the abolition of the unit fines system and a tougher sentencing policy all round.

Symptomatic of the new political climate – note that it has nothing whatever to do with the issue of how much crime is being committed – was the speech by Home Secretary Kenneth Clarke to the House of Commons in May 1993:

> We will seek to amend section one of the 1991 act to allow the courts to take into account all the offences for which the offender has been convicted or for which he has been dealt with – instead of only one offence, or that offence and one other offence, which is the case now ... We propose to restore to the courts their power to have full regard to the criminal record of an offender and his response to previous sentences when deciding on the sentence for his current offences.[20]

The net result is that prison musters are on the rise. In the first 11 months of 1993 the overall prison population increased by 6547 (16 percent), an average increase of nearly 600 per month. The number of remand prisoners rose by 3613 (44 percent) and the number of young prisoners aged under 21 rose by 1505 (22 percent). This rate of increase over such a short period is unprecedented in recent years.[21] These figures include 845 people jailed for an average of two weeks each for failing to pay their television licence fee of £83 pounds ($NZ200). One-third of these – 292 – were women, most of them from single-parent families.[22]

It now appears that in 1995-96 an additional 4200 offenders (over and above the previously projected increase) will be imprisoned, and an extra 5000 by the end of the decade.

Remands in custody are also on the increase. By January 1994 more than a quarter of people in custody were on remand. More than 60 percent of those people will not subsequently receive a jail sentence.[23] It is clear that judges, magistrates and justices of the peace have got a lot tougher on conditions for bail as the political rhetoric on law and order has grown. Yet the Prison Reform Trust claims that re-offending while on bail, the supposed cause of this increase, is no higher now than it was 10 years ago.[24]

As a further sign of the hardening of the government's already punitive arteries, the Home Office has quashed a special 15-point programme designed to help probation services deal with domestic violence, the special needs of the children of women offenders, and petty women criminals in prison. Proposed government research into race issue (blacks are about seven times more likely to be imprisoned than whites) has also been rejected.

A major result of this new tough-line policy has been the abandonment of the first national programme for helping women offenders. A strategic policy for all 55 probation services in England and Wales, drawn up by representatives of the Home Office and probation executives, called for probation officers to become aware of the dangers of courts labelling women as irrational and mentally ill, to consider whether families could afford the fines imposed, and to take the claims of the victims of domestic violence seriously. Home Officer Minister Donald McLean labelled the programmes 'too politically correct' and, amid outrage, scrapped them.[25]

Ironically, two of the three latest Home Secretaries (Justice Ministers) were themselves convicted of law-breaking in court decisions handed down in November 1994. The High Court ruled that Douglas Hurd, who had introduced the White Paper in 1990, acted unlawfully in authorising aid for a controversial Malaysian dam project. The court upheld an unprecedented appeal against a £234 million ($NZ607m) subsidised loan that the British government admitted became 'entangled' with a huge British arms deal with Malaysia. The government is required by the judgment to make good the £25 million a year deficiency in the aid budget caused by the loan.

In the Appeal Court, hard-line Minister Michael Howard, who scuttled the progressive elements that flowed from Hurd's White Paper, was judged '... to have acted unlawfully, abused his power, and flouted the will of Parliament' in cutting compensation for crime victims.

British prisons have again become overcrowded, violent cesspools of humanity in which, as Brendan O'Friel observed at Strangeways, the weak will become 'contaminated' by the wicked. They will be degraded by the conditions meted out to them by a vindictive Parliament spurred on by a media war for sales. Already British prisons have come under scrutiny by their European neighbours, who generally speaking treat their prisoners much more humanely and imprison far fewer per head of population.

A Council of Europe Committee in a special report on three British prisons slammed the authorities for the conditions in which they held prisoners. It said that the direct result of the inadequate regime activities was that many prisoners routinely spent practically the whole of the day locked in their cells. Prisoners alleged, and it was confirmed by prison officers and governor-grade staff, that out-of-cell time during a 24-hour period was on occasion as little as one to two hours and frequently less than four hours. The condition of unconvicted prisoners as regards regime activities tended to be even less favourable than that of the convicted prisoners.[26]

Overcrowding results in cramped and unpleasant physical conditions. It also results in restricted regimes, as overcrowded prisons do not have the space, the facilities or the resources to provide prisoners with a full range of training, work and educational opportunities when they have too many prisoners to cater for properly. Overcrowding is not only a recipe for re-offending upon release. It is also a recipe for rioting in prisons, as it increases frustration among those forced to live cheek by jowl in cramped conditions.[27]

The Chief Inspector of Prisons in England and Wales inspected Wandsworth Prison in London in April 1989. The prison held about 1500 male prisoners; its usual capacity is 1254. The Chief Inspector found that prisoners were issued with one bucket or bowl and one towel. They used these for all their personal washing and also for washing their plates, knives and forks. Not all prisoners had a bath or shower each week. The shower room was described by the Chief Inspector as 'a ghastly place with the atmosphere of an earlier century'.

In the segregation unit, where prisoners were isolated either for punishment or for their own protection, there was no opportunity to empty their lavatory buckets from 2.30pm until the following morning. Some prisoners did not get clean clothes for two or three weeks and were not able to wash their clothes themselves. Racial harassment of black prison inmates was also reported. The Chief Inspector concluded in his report:

> For prisoners, life at Wandsworth was a deadening experience broken only by conversation about routines or a future life of crime.[28]

Pentonville, in North London, which dates from 1842 and has about 650 inmates, was in March 1994 also the subject of a scathing attack by the Chief Inspector of Prisons, Judge Stephen Tumim. He described health-care facilities as 'grossly inadequate, run-down, cramped, dirty and unfit for patients'. His report described the 55 asylum-seekers and refugees incarcerated as being 'distressed, despondent and in some cases desperate'.[29]

Prison officers also suffer from the tensions and frustrations of an overcrowded system. The chairman of the Prison Officers' Association in November 1993 after the parliamentary changes referred to 'a prison service facing an eruption of violence':

> If proof were needed of how serious the crisis has become, the Director-general has himself provided it. He has publicly warned that a continued increase in prison numbers will lead to more rioting.

I have a message for the Director-general, his Prison Board and Ministers [of the government]. The next time there is a riot, join us at the sharp end. Fall in with the control and restraint squad. Feel the sickening void in your stomach. Experience the absolute reliance on your fellow officer born out of years of service and experience. Feel the comradeship of standing shoulder to shoulder whilst facing the violent life-threatening mob intent on inflicting crippling injury. You will all find it an enlightening experience having to sort out the mess you created in the first place.[30]

Conclusion

Things have changed a bit in Ripon now. The old prison closed down in 1877. Did the Home Secretary who ordered its closure recognise that retribution was an ineffective and dehumanising way of treating human beings? Regrettably, the philosophy did not die with him. Retributive justice is alive and kicking in 1990s Britain.

Just how morally bankrupt and practically inept Britain's penal policy has become can be seen in the latest efforts to house its burgeoning prison population. In December 1993 plans were revealed for prison ships to be moored at Birkenhead and Barrow-in-Furness to cope with the expected surge in prison population – a return to the hulk days! Permanent prison ships have not been used in Britain since 1778 when old men-of-war were last used to house prisoners.

The contingency plans were contained in a memorandum to the Home Secretary from the Director-general of Prisons, and are required to meet the 5000 increase in prison musters as a result of the government's U-turn over the Criminal Justice Act, which gave courts greater discretion in sentencing.

Tony Christopher, the chairman of NACRO, said at the time that it was it was a matter of great regret that there has been such a hasty and ill-considered retreat from some of the principles of the 1991 Criminal Justice Act. The criminal justice system is being seen as a solution for a range of social problems. Prosecuting more people, taking them through the courts and imprisoning them will not solve the problems of homelessness, unemployment, family breakdown, and educational under-achievement. What was desperately needed was the intelligent treatment of causes.[31]

The true concerns of justice, according to Adrian Speller, are the establishment, maintenance and restoration of right relations within the community.[32] For a nation to expect its criminal justice system (and its penal section in particular) to somehow right massive wrongs in the social relationships of a community is ridiculous, and wrong. It simply cannot be done and is a cop-out for local council and central government policy-makers.

Britain continues to apply a demonstrably failed retributive philosophy to its criminal justice system. The vitriolic rantings of the tabloids feed the insatiable dark side of the British psyche. The public seeks simplistic solutions to complex social problems, including crime.

Yet despite hundreds of years of punishment and vengeance, crime is on the increase. Twice as many British people now commit crime as they did 40 years ago. Prison has solved nothing. It has simply proved beyond a shadow of a doubt that it plays a major role in ensuring a continued high level of crime and criminal behaviour.

The trumpet call for vengeance and punishment remains loud and clear throughout the land; the scapegoating of the poor is as alive and kicking. The failed philosophy of Ripon has entered the very psyche of British national consciousness and the events of the past few years show it to be well entrenched.

Footnotes

1. *The Tablet*, London, 27 November 1993
2. Report, 'Relational Justice – A New Approach to Penal Reform', Jubilee Policy Group and Prison Fellowship, England and Wales, in association with the Prison Service Chaplaincy, Cambridge, December 1992, pp9-10
3. Ibid, pp10-11
4. Vivien Stern, paper on 'Crime, Policy and the Role of Punishment', 19 April 1993
5. Ibid
6. Catholic Social Welfare Commission report, 'A Time for Justice', 1982
7. Vivien Stern, op cit
8. Adrian Speller, *Breaking Out*, Hodder and Stoughton, London, 1986,
9. NACRO annual report, 1992-93
10. Vivien Stern, op cit
11. *The Guardian*, 24 June 1994
12. Vivien Stern, Allan Nixon Memorial Lecture, Auckland, New Zealand, June 1990
13. Ibid
14. *Trends in Crime and their Interpretation: A Study in Recorded Crime in England and Wales*, Home Office, 1990
15. White Paper, *Crime, Justice and Protecting the Public*, February 1990, House of Commons, England.
16. Ibid 2.4
17. Ibid 2.7
18. Ibid 4.10
19. Ibid 2.8
20. Paper: *Criminal Justice Act 1991: Its Impact on Services*, NACRO, 1993
21. Ibid
22. *The Independent on Sunday*, 13 March 1994
23. *The Times*, 30 May 1994
24. *The Independent*, 30 May 1994
25. *The Independent on Sunday*, 13 March 1994
26. Paper, 'Notes on Overcrowding', NACRO, 1993
27. Ibid
28. Report on HM Prison, Wandsworth, by HM Chief Inspector of Prisons, Home Office, London 1989
29. *The Independent*, 22 March 1994
30. 'Notes on Overcrowding', op cit
31. Tony Christopher, NACRO, 1993
32. Adrian Speller, op cit

CHAPTER FIVE

The Caging of America

Various kinds of state-sponsored torture and abuse – of the kind ingeniously designed to cause pain but without a telltale 'significant injury' – lashing prisoners with leather straps, whipping them with rubber hoses, beating them with naked fists, shocking them with electric currents, asphyxiating them short of death, intentionally exposing them to undue heat or cold, or forcibly injecting them with psychosis-inducing drugs – techniques, commonly thought to be practised outside this nation's borders, are hardly unknown within this nation's prisons.

Supreme Court Justice Harry A. Blackmun
Hudson vs McMillian, 25 February 1992

The United States has a very violent culture. The modern state was born in violence, raised on conquest. The indigenous peoples were devastated first by disease, then by brute force. The environment was 'tamed', vast landscapes mutilated. A civil war took 365,000 lives.

The gun has become the symbol of that violence, a symbol of the culture itself. Firearms kill about 34,000 Americans every year. There are as many Americans killed by domestic guns at home in any 18-month period as died in the whole of the Vietnam War. Belfast in Northern Ireland has been a much safer place to live than New York, Chicago or the violence capital of the world, Washington DC.

Thomas Jefferson High School is a solid red-orange brick block building set down in the East New York neighbourhood of boarded-up row houses. In the four years 1988-91, some 70 students were killed, shot, stabbed or permanently injured on the school grounds. According to a report prepared for the New York State Assembly and quoted by the New York *Daily News*, 50 percent of the 1900 students have some kind of puncture wound on their body at any given time. The school maintains a burial fund to help families with the funeral expenses.

According to *Time* (9 March 1992), the United States has always had a gun culture. Now gun violence has metastasised in a new way among the young. The gun becomes neighbourhood logic, rite of passage, administrator, avenger, instrument of impulse and rough justice. When guns reach critical mass they take on a malignant life of their own. Gun violence is spreading like Aids, not just in New York City but in Los Angeles and Houston and Boston and other cities as well. In the past four years, arrests for homicides among juveniles have gone up 93 percent, compared with a 16 percent increase among adults. The children of the baby-boomers are arriving at the crime-prone teen years, and too many of them are packing firearms. Criminologists are predicting more increases in homicides in the next few years.

Guns have a sort of irresistible black magic about them. A good gun has such a lovely heft, a densely sinister weight in the hand. The brain is wired to the trigger finger and fires on impulse. The finger twitches, and – blam! – the target disintegrates: an existence powdered. The finger did it on a whim. The casualisation of life, a society of emotional disconnection. Killing is a kind of dream-sequence video where conscience is disconnected from trigger finger, child is disconnected from future. Bullet is disconnected from gun muzzle and, once fired, can never be recalled.[1]

The lifestyle of the nation is reinforced by a military force, the largest in history, still with an armed capacity of 1.8 million men and women. The Defence Department spent $279 billion in 1993-94.[2] The government also exported $41 billion in arms sales and military assistance during this period. This makes the United States far and away the world's largest manufacturer and exporter of arms.[3]

The violence of its culture spills over into its criminal justice system and in particular into its prisons. Nowhere in the world are people jailed as quickly, as often, or for as long as in the United States. Their rate of imprisonment is approximately four times that of New Zealand, which trails well behind in second place.

Perhaps nowhere is the violence of the culture more marked in the US than by the acceptance of up to 80 percent of the population of the death penalty. More than 270 prisoners have been executed since 1976, when deliberate death by the state was again declared to be constitutional. Recent federal legislative changes add more than 50 fresh offences to those already carrying the death penalty and more than 3000 prisoners await execution. Most are black, poor, young, male and have been poorly represented by state-assigned lawyers at their trials.

Interestingly, in April 1994, Supreme Court Justice Harry Blackmun, who had upheld death sentences throughout a lengthy term on the court that had seen 228 people executed, declared his opposition to all death-penalty laws.

> Rather than continue to coddle the court's delusion that the desired level of fairness has been achieved and the need for regulations eviscerated, I feel morally and intellectually obliged simply to point out that the death-penalty experiment has failed. It seems that the decision whether a human being should live or die is

so inherently subjective, rife with all of life's understandings, experiences, pre-
judices and passions, that it inevitably defies the rationality and consistency
required by the Constitution.[4]

The Cold, Hard Facts

There are three principal prison systems in the US. At the county and city level is
a system of jails. At the state level is a system of state prisons. And interspersed
within every state is a comprehensive system of federal prisons.

In 1968 the prison population of the US was 188,000. By 1991 there were a
total of 823,414 Americans in state or federal prisons, which, coupled with the
426,479 in local jails, brought the nation's tally of imprisoned people to
1,249,893. The total in state and federal prisons has increased 150 percent
between 1980 and 1991 and the 1995 total is expected to be 1.5 million. In the
eight years 1984-92 the imprisonment rate for people of colour – Hispanics, Afro-
Americans, Native Americans – has nearly doubled.

Currently 0.5 percent of the total US population is behind bars, a number that
increases by about 13 percent per annum. In 1992, 4.4 million citizens lived under
correctional supervision of one form or another, which is around 2 percent of the
population.

Seven states – California, Colorado, Connecticut, Kentucky, Michigan, New
Hampshire and New Jersey – doubled their male prison populations in just six
years between 1986 and 1991.[5] In addition 3.2 million adults, about 1.7 percent of
all American residents, were on parole or probation.[6]

As Vivien Stern of NACRO, the British National Association for the Care and
Resettlement of Offenders, points out:

> In 1992 in the city of Chicago 1200 people were murdered. A young American
> man is 20 times more likely to be murdered than a young English or Danish
> man. A black boy born today in the state of California has a greater chance of
> being murdered in his lifetime than of attending the University of California.
> This is not happening because there are no police in the United States, no courts
> or prisons. It is not happening because they have short sentences and let people
> 'walk free' from court with a community service order.
>
> On the contrary, the sentencing is some of the hardest in the world. Many
> commentators would say it is happening because of social policies which have
> been followed in the US for the past three decades. It is sometimes difficult to
> draw concrete links between social policy and crime, but it is inescapable. Many
> questions about the relationship between crime and social policy are unanswered,
> but the weight of evidence internationally points to certain propositions.
> Weakening community support structures, reducing opportunities for young
> people, widening inequalities and leaving vulnerable families to fend for
> themselves will lead to crime.[7]

These facts are borne out by the insight contained in the Report of the National Commission on the Causes and Prevention of Violence. Chaired by Milton Eisenhower in 1969, it reported:

> To be a young poor male; to be under-educated, without means of escape from an oppressive urban environment; to want what society claims is available (but mostly to others); to see around oneself illegitimate and often violent methods used to achieve material gain; and to observe others using these means with impunity – all this is to be burdened with an enormous set of influences that pull many toward crimes and delinquency.

If present trends continue, the numbers of American citizens in prison will double by the year 2000, when there will be more than 2 million incarcerated.

Yet some crime indicators signalled that criminal offending was down. The Uniform Crime Reports Index (UCR) fell by 2 percent over the period 1980-90. This is the index supplied by the FBI, an index of crimes for which official police reports have been filed. And 'victimisation rates' as charted by the National Crime Survey (NCS) fell by 20 percent. This is measured by the Bureau of the Census of the Justice Department.[8]

Crime among those younger than 18 years old has edged up within the last 20 years, but, according to FBI figures, the overall crime rate during that time has shown little or no growth. Robbery is down 46 percent over the past 20 years, and theft is down 35 percent. The number of rapes has increased, partially because rape is now reported much more often than before.[9]

The official Justice Department figures (as distinct from the FBI), however, showed a crime rise of 7.3 percent in the decade 1980-90, while the imprisonment rate doubled.[10] By 1992, 1142 new prison cells were being required each week to keep up.[11] By the year 2000, corrections expenditure may cost $40 billion per year, 20 times their cost in 1975.[12]

Ironically there is more public money spent trying to deal with crime than is lost from criminal activity. The US now spends more than $21 billion a year on construction and maintenance of prisons. (*Time*, 17 May 1994). In 1985 society lost an estimated $10 billion from crime, but more than $50 billion was spent on activities related to criminal justice. More than half the people imprisoned committed crimes that involved less than $1000. At the same time, 40 US corporations with combined profits of more than $10 billion paid no federal income tax at all.[14]

At least 60 percent of violent crime is associated with drug use. Addicts commit 15 times as many robberies and 20 times as many burglaries as criminals who are not on drugs. Approximately 70 percent of America's prisoners have drug problems.

Widespread Criminality

Criminality reaches from the bottom to the very top of American society. The Nixon Watergate and Clinton Whitewater scandals have been only the tip of what must be seen as one of the most corrupt and violent types of administration in the democratic Western world. In recent years many top officials have been jailed for corruption, including several cabinet ministers. Outgoing presidents often pardon colleagues under investigation for varying degrees of criminality.

The latest is certainly not unique. In January 1994 a special investigation found both previous United States presidents, Ronald Reagan and George Bush, to have been:

> ... well-briefed cheerleaders of the Iran-Contra scandal operations in the 1980s, [who] conspired to cover up their support of crimes committed by others.

Special prosecutor Laurence Walsh in his report insisted they knew about the overall illegal schemes to sell arms to Muslim revolutionary Iran and resupply Nicaraguan Contra rebels in 1985 and 1986. Both denied all allegations.

George Bush is the man who used the Willie Horton mugshots campaign of promising tough sentences for law-breakers to defeat Michael Dukakis and win the 1988 presidential election. Horton was a convicted murderer and Massachusetts prisoner on parole from prison when he committed a sexual assault. This is the same president who vowed to crack down on law-breakers and 'take back the streets by taking criminals off them'. True to his word, he was clearly the toughest US president on street crime that the nation had ever seen.

One of the major reasons there are so many in prison is that there are now more than 100 federal laws whose violation requires a mandatory prison sentence. Drug offences constitute the largest of this group. There are now more people in prison for drug offences that there are for crimes of property.[13] Such federal law changes were a favourite tactic of Bush. This is the president who found time to pardon his former Defence Secretary, Casper Weinberger, and other officials as one of his last acts in office.

His type of political hypocrisy is symptomatic of similar political rhetoric around the world. The fact that the Willie Horton campaign led to a tightening of prison paroles for hundreds of thousands of law-abiding inmates quietly 'doing their time' did not seem to worry him. In the previous year, 200,000 home leaves had been granted to 50,000 inmates, 99 percent of whom never offended while on parole. Because of Bush's electioneering in 1988, tighter controls mean that tens of thousands fewer are eligible for paroles.

The US now imprisons at a rate of 520 per 100,000, four times that of New Zealand, five time that of Britain, six times that of Australia, 16 times that of Ireland, and 25 times that of the Philippines. In 1970 the US rate was 97 per

100,000 population. In less than 25 years it has increased by 530 percent. The two men most responsible for this horrendous escalation are Ronald Reagan and George Bush, both now accused of law-breaking themselves.

US Prisons Are Brutal

Prison rape is as American as apple pie. In September 1982, *Time* ran a special report on US prisons, describing them as a mess, with punishments ranging from the purgatorial to the hellish.

In a well-designed progressive place a five-year-term is with luck just that: five years of life terribly circumscribed, with all but a few personal choices and pleasures denied. But in many other prisons, implicit in the same nominal term are five years of extortion and knives; bodies grabbed and ransacked; a sour filthy cell shared for most of the day with a hothead who would not mind killing again. The experience of a given prison is indiscriminate. The car thief endures the same, day by day, as the angeldust wholesaler and the habitual stomper of young schoolchildren.

In the 1991 'Human Rights Watch Report on Prison Conditions in the United States' it is noted that:

> ... perhaps the most troubling aspect of the human-rights situation in US prisons is a trend we observed that could be labelled 'Marionization'. In 1983 the federal prison at Marion, Illinois, implemented a series of extraordinary security measures. Since then 36 states have followed in creating their own super-maximum-security institutions.

Writing in the *Catholic Worker*, (March-April 1993), Bonnie Kerness noted that the confinement in these units is administered by prison officials without independent supervision and leads to a situation in which inmates may in fact be sentenced twice: once by the court, and the second time by the prison administration to particularly harsh conditions:

> Prisoners are placed in a cage in a human warehouse where they will eat, sleep, exercise, wash, read, think and take care of bodily functions. They are there for 24 hours a day, day in and day out, year in and year out. There is a huge steel door between each and the outside world. Perhaps each may be allowed out twice a week for an hour or two of recreation, and may be allowed a 15-minute phone call a day. The phone calls are monitored, reading material censored.
>
> If for some reason an inmate has to leave the cell, he or she is strip-searched, which often includes a humiliating anal probe. Each will be shackled around the waist and handcuffed. The food may be tampered with, while medical care may be non-existent. The inmate is totally under the control of mainly white-supremacist prison guards, whose hatred of them and their beliefs soon becomes abundantly clear. One must remain constantly on the alert against mental and

physical deterioration. In effect such prisons are used as social-control mechanisms. They serve political functions.[15]

The inhumanity of the American penal system is hard to believe. Cold prison statistics hide the harsh reality of life behind bars in the United States. The opening quote to this chapter from Supreme Court Justice Harry A. Blackmun says it all. He refers to state-sponsored torture and abuse, lashings, whippings, beatings, electric shocks, asphyxiation and enforced drug-taking. Violence in the culture breeds violent offenders, who meet violence in prison and return to the community more violent than ever. That is what the statistics say. That is what the facts reveal.

At the Public Safety Building in Syracuse in upstate New York, the prison that housed New Zealand Ploughshares peace activist Moana Cole for a period in 1991, inmates are tortured. A report in the *National Catholic Reporter* in October 1992 claimed that prisoners were handcuffed to the bars of their cells for days at a time.

In Washington DC the Prisoners' Legal Services Project tracks systematic and personal violations of the basic rights of prisoners. The chaining of the legs of women in labour is one practice they took to court and had stopped. They have recorded many cases of prisoners taken to hospitals sick and dying, and their families are only informed after their deaths.

Sociologist Greg Newbold, who visited US prisons in Nebraska, Tennessee, New Orleans, California, Nevada and Maryland, estimates that in up to a third of prisons in the US inmates are kept 'third-world conditions'.[16] In 1990 there were 56 murders in penal institutions and thousands of serious assaults.[17] In 40 states and the District of Columbia, courts have ruled that prison conditions violate federal or state constitutions.[18] This means their conditions do not meet minimum standards fit for human beings.

Vivien Stern of NACRO in London talks of a prisoner in the United States who corresponds with her office:

He probably spends most of his day locked up underground with chains between his legs and chained to four other prisoners. He has his food passed through a slot and he's probably allowed out of his cell for an hour a day if he is on the regime that affects many of the people in his prison. There are prisons like that being built all over the United States to house the people who cause trouble in other prisons. Perhaps they've got five life sentences and no remission and there's no reason for them not to cause trouble.[19]

According to the *New Internationalist* (March 1992), beatings of prisoners are routine during cell transfers. Rectal probes are said to be used to intimidate and rape prisoners moved out of certain high-security prisons. The loss of privileges and withdrawal of visiting rights by families are routinely used to intimidate prisoners.

Brutality reeks from every encounter one has with the penal system in the United States, be it in a local county jail, a state prison or a federal one. Handcuffs and leg irons are routine. Moana Cole, who weights just 45kg and was in prison for peaceful non-violent actions, was handcuffed and put in chains to visit a dentist in the local town. Leg irons were clapped around her ankles. The chains from these led to her waist where there was a leather belt, with further chains to her cuffed hands. Two guards had to support her getting in and out of the dental chair. Prior to this she had to wait in a crowded waiting room for her turn. Ciaron O'Reilly, her co-defendant, was flown several thousand kilometres to a prison in Texas in handcuffs and chains. This reflects a system built on violence and humiliation, not respect for human dignity.

Conditions have deteriorated markedly for women in prison as inmate numbers have risen. In 1993 there were 55,365 women in federal or state prisons, up from 12,200 in 1980. Half of these women were black and two-thirds had had children before they were 18 years old. They are nearly all in jail for drug possession or sale, prostitution or money crimes. About 10 percent of the women admitted to prison are pregnant, 80 percent or 40,000 of them are mothers, and virtually all were the sole support for their children.

Professor Sean McCouville, a professor of criminal justice in Illinois, says that among the biggest problems facing American prison administrators are prison gangs, assaults, rape and the extortion of the weak inmates by the tougher ones.[20] The number of men raped in US prisons each day may exceed 25,000. Women, who make up 4 percent of the prison population, also suffer rape and abuse daily.

According to *Prison Law Monitor*, one in five prisoners is raped.[21] Tom Cahill, a specialist in the field of prison rape, says prison rapists typically victimise young heterosexual first offenders. He claims the boredom, frustration, sexism, racism and outright terror combine to create an atmosphere of barbarism behind bars.[22]

Rape is simply a fruit of the violent ethic that pervades American prisons. Deaths, stabbings, beatings, riots and suicides make up the everyday diet of many institutions. In a two-year period in the early 1980s, 225 inmates and 11 guards were killed by other inmates, and inmate suicides totalled 263. The pattern has been maintained into the 1990s, with 54 inmates and two guards killed in 1990.[23]

Brutality breeds brutality. A classic case occurred on 3 February 1980, when the pent-up rage of inmates in the penitentiary of New Mexico near Sante Fe finally erupted. Home to 1157 inmates, it had embraced a harsh regime meant to teach the inmates a lesson.

Then the riot broke out and mayhem resulted. They set mattresses alight. They used acetylene torches to cut into 'snitch' cellblocks they had been unable to unlock, and once inside they used the torches to cut into the cells of their intended victims. The caged men, unable to escape, were defenceless. The rioting prisoners chopped off one man's head with a shovel. They used the acetylene torch on another man's genitals, then burned his eyes out. They pounded an iron bar into one man's ear, and kept pounding until it came out of the other side of his skull. They sprayed lighter fluid into a cell, set it alight and watched as the man inside burned to death in the inferno. They raped and stabbed men, beat them with baseball bats and steel pipes, threw them over the railing and down to the concrete floor from the second-storey tier.

The 24-year-old New Mexico penitentiary smouldered, its concrete walls having mostly failed the night before to muffle the screams of men who were being hacked, stabbed, hanged, burned and beaten to death.

The bodies were still inside. So were several hundred inmates, many of them wounded and choking in the dense smoke. Others, maniacally smeared with blood, stalked the open corridors, carrying baseball bats and steel pipes. A handful of guards – some of them naked, bound with ropes and repeatedly raped – lay traumatised and injured in the filth.

When the riot finally ended later on the second day, there would be 33 dead, 90 injured, $20 million in damage. It had been 36 hours of wanton slaughter and mindless mayhem. In terms of death, it was the nation's second-worst prison riot in modern times. In terms of damage it was quite possibly the costliest in prison history. In terms of brutality, it was unsurpassed.[24]

One of the major causes of the riot was a policy change by administrators. In the 1970s many of the prison's programmes and projects were abandoned in favour of a hard-line stance against inmates. The 'get tough' policy saw political decisions, a lack of consistency in rules, the unpredictability of the guards and arbitrary punishment succeed in weakening the hold of programme-orientated inmates, who had exerted a stabilising influence on the others. When education and activity programmes began to fall by the wayside, the power base of those inmate leaders was eroded. Power in the prison passed instead to those whose creed was violence.

Racist as Well
Civil rights were won for Afro-Americans more than two decades ago. But what was won in the legislature is lost daily in the courtrooms. Across the country, blacks have their basic right to a fair trial and good representation trampled on by the demons of a racist criminal justice system. Mandatory prison terms for many offences mean that hundreds of thousands more are now penalised unjustly in the prison system than were ever penalised in the worst days of discrimination.

The figures prove the racism of the justice system. While the 1994 national average is 520 people going to prison for every 100,000 population, for blacks it is over 800. They now comprise 45 percent of the federal and state prison population (nearly double the 23 percent of 1925), making up 61 percent of incarcerated juveniles, and 42 percent of inmates on death row.

In 1986 some 609,690 black men were under the control of the criminal justice system, while only 436,000 were enrolled in college.[25]

These figure are merely the tip of the iceberg. Each one represents a person with a life story. Every prisoners' rights groups in the country tells the same story. The defendants are all poor. Most have had court-appointed attorneys for their cases, many of whom are white middle-class graduates of law school anxious to gain a little experience, but not necessarily committed to their client's wellbeing. The net result is a mountain of horror stories of poorly defended young blacks going to prison and even to death row after minimum defence in what amounts to a sham of a hearing.

As Bonnie Kerness writes, if you are poor, young, male and of African descent in the US and you get arrested, your bail is likely to be set so high that you become an economic hostage. The phrase 'innocent until proven guilty' will have little meaning. You will sit in a cell for up to two years without even having been found guilty of anything. You will certainly not get a trial by a jury of your peers, and you are quite likely to be pressured into forgoing your right to a trial altogether. You will be defended by a poorly paid public defender who has a caseload so vast that you cannot possibly be treated as a priority. Finally, you will receive a sentence 30 percent longer than a white person would receive for the same crime. You have seen the same thing happen to your father, your uncles, or your cousins.[26]

Nationwide about 25 percent of all black males will be in the criminal justice system at some time. In Washington DC, home of the US president, the Congress and the Supreme Court, close to half of all black men will see the inside of a prison before they reach the age of 24.[27]

A typical case is that of black activist journalist Mumia Abu-Jamal, convicted in 1982 by an all-white jury of the shooting death of a Philadelphia police officer. At the time he was president of the Philadelphia Association of Black Journalists, and the local newspaper, the *Philadelphia Inquirer*, had called him 'the voice of the voiceless'. His hard-hitting investigative journalism had challenged police brutality, especially against the black community.

Over 125 eyewitnesses saw the shooting and from them the police chose two, both with previous convictions and pending charges, as the key prosecution witnesses. Some of the other eyewitnesses reported seeing someone else shoot the officer and flee. One defence witness testified that she and one of the state's witnesses were offered a deal to identify him as the shooter.

His trial was presided over by Judge Albert Sabo, notorious for sentencing more people to death than any other judge in the country. Mumia Abu-Jamal was allotted $150 by the court to prepare his defence from his prison cell. He was barred from representing himself, and the judge forced an unprepared attorney to represent the defendant. When Mumia protested that this was unfair, he was banished from much of the trial.

Thousands of people from every state, including many prominent jurists, along with 40 members of the Pennsylvania Legislature, have concluded that he did not have a fair trial. Yet Mumia Abu-Jamal remains on death row. How many more hundreds like him face the same penalty but without the backup of a public campaign?

Canadian Quaker and international prison abolitionist Ruth Morris says that taking the racism out of criminal justice systems would be like taking the religion out of churches or the sex out of marriage – it cannot be done because the major thing justice systems exist for is to maintain racial and class systems and barriers. Retributive justice, classism and racism are like Siamese triplets. You cannot change any of them without affecting the others because retributive justice systems exist mainly to reinforce the racial and class strata in our society.[28]

Three Strikes and You're Out

American criminal law is getting tougher by the day as legislators seek re-election in the 1990s riding on the back of the widespread fear in American society of violent crime in the community.

Early in 1994 California passed the Jones-Costa Three Strikes Law. It is generally referred to as the 'three strikes and you're out' law, a phrase taken from baseball terminology. Its goal is to put repeat offenders into prison for sentences of 25 years to life without possibility of parole. The law will imprison for life any defendant who is convicted for a third offence if that person has two previous violence convictions – even if the third conviction is for a non-violent felony such as passing a bad cheque.[29]

A network of underwriters, builders and correction officers has a powerful financial interest in perpetuating and expanding the boom in the prison industry. One group of the beneficiaries, the prison guards of California, contributed $1 million to help Republican Pete Wilson become governor. In return, the governor initiated the most expansive prison construction programme any state has ever undertaken. He has also approved the guards' request for more benefits.[30]

The implications of this action for the rest of the United States has been horrific. The 'domino theory' is alive and well. Within months, 16 other states had debated and/or implemented similar 'three strikes' measures, and so had the federal government. All of this will lead to the same boom expansion of the penal industrial complex.

The Californian legislation was the model. Basically it has three provisions. For first-time felony offenders, the statute leaves intact the prior-sentencing guideline. For second-time offenders, the new law doubles the minimum required sentence. The centrepiece of the legislation is its 'three strikes' provision, which mandates that state courts sentence to an 'indeterminate term of life imprisonment' those individuals previously convicted for two or more serious and/or violent felonies. While the rhetoric implies a life sentence without possibility of parole, in effect a convicted three-time felon will now have to serve triple the first-time sentence, with a minimum of 25 years' imprisonment.[31]

The influential *Harvard Law Review* took issue with three interrelated concerns. First, the statute's definition of a 'strike' treats many property crimes just like violent crimes. This is a very imprecise method of targeting violent dangerous offenders, at whom the law was principally aimed.

The new law extends its reach to the sentencing of non-violent offenders. For instance, a two-time cheque forger caught committing a non-violent residential burglary must now receive a life term in prison.

Second, the statute does not promote long-term crime prevention because it fails to cope with the socioeconomic roots of California's crime problem. 'Three strikes' in effect adopts an approach that maintains the boundaries of economic and social segregation. Whereas harsh sentences for *violent* felonies could work to protect all communities, harsh sentences for *economic* crimes work mainly to reinforce the economic insulation of California's suburban neighbourhoods.

Third, implementing the statute will saddle California with huge economic costs that will further undermine long-term prevention goals.[32]

Prison musters in the state, which were running in the early 1990s at around 120,000, will rise to nearly 400,000 over the next five years at an extra cost of $US2 billion per year. The 20 new prisons required will cost an estimated $US21 billion.[33]

This madness does not stop in California. Riding on the back of that state's legislation and facing imminent mid-term elections for both houses of Congress and numerous governorships, the US Senate and House of Representatives in August 1994 passed a crime bill worth an extra $US30 billion that would create scores of new federal crimes. The bill was described by its proponents as the most ambitious anti-crime bill in the past 50 years. It provided money to put 100,000 more police on the streets through to the year 2000, and nearly $US10 billion for new prison construction.

It included lifetime imprisonment for three-time violent offenders – the 'three strikes and you're out' provision. It made 58 new federal crimes subject to the death penalty. The legislation contained such proposals as boot camps, and new draconian penalties for people involved in drugs. The new legislation will increase the federal prison population by 50 percent by the year 2000, when 60 percent of all inmates will be drug offenders.[34]

Prior to its passage an American Civil Liberties Union memo concluded that life under the federal crime bill would be frightening to imagine. It contemplated a society where large segments would be disposable; where executions and the death penalty would be broadly and deeply entrenched into the national consciousness; where an overwhelming number of the Afro-American population would be imprisoned; where 13-year-olds could be herded off to serve mandatory sentences of 20 years or more; where people could be plucked off the streets for wearing certain (gang) colours; and where teachers would be required to report on pupils.[35]

Conclusion

The retributive criminal justice system prevalent in the United States reflects the deep roots of a violent culture. It is difficult to see how anything other than a total revolution of values can turn this death culture and its justice system around.

Whichever way we look at it, the well-meaning experiment by American Quakers to develop the penitentiary as a way of reforming criminals has backfired horribly. The United States is quickly becoming a caged society, with fear of crime imprisoning more and more of those who are not already incarcerated.

The American criminal justice system is now so adversarial that actually getting some sort of justice is incidental to the process. At this moment, 1.4 million American citizens are in prison and the numbers are skyrocketing. Naturally not all the prisons are as harsh and brutal as some referred to in this chapter. Some states make prison life tolerable, some even quite humane. Wisconsin and Minnesota are two states that have a tradition of progressive penal policy.

Regrettably such states are in a minority. Retribution and vengeance are at the heart of the nation's approach to crime and punishment. As Barry Krisberg, president of the National Council on Crime and Delinquency, says: 'Punitive responses are embedded in the American psyche.'[36]

It is this revolution of values, from the violent to the non-violent, from the punitive and vengeful to the healing and merciful, from the fragmented to the holistic, that is contained in a restorative philosophy and expounded in the chapters that follow.

Footnotes

1. *Time*, 9 March 1992
2. *National Catholic Reporter*, 1 October 1993
3. *National Catholic Reporter*, 20 September 1991
4. *National Catholic Reporter*, 22 April 1994
5. *Bureau of Justice Statistics Bulletin*, 1992
6. *Bureau of Statistics Bulletin Update*, January 1992
7. Vivien Stern, 'Crime Policy and the Role of Punishment', *RSA Journal*, October 1993, p700
8. *Economist*, London. 17 November 1993
9. *National Catholic Reporter*, 24 December 1993
10. *Sojourners*, 12 June 1990
11. *National Catholic Reporter*, 13 August 1993
12. John J. Di Iulio, *No Escape, the Future of American Corrections*, Basic Books, New York, 1991
13. *New Internationalist*, December 1985
14. *National Catholic Reporter*, 13 August 1993
15. *Time*, 13 September 1982
16. *Christchurch Mail*, 23 August 1993
17. *New Internationalist*, March 1992
18. *National Catholic Reporter*, 13 August 1985
19. Vivien Stern, op cit, p703
20. *Christchurch Star*, 8 March 1985
21. *The Progressive*, November 1985
22. Ibid
23. *Christchurch Mail,* 23 August 1993
24. *Albuquerque Journal*, 3 February 1985
25. 'Young Black Men and the Criminal Justice System – A Growing National Problem, Sentencing Project, Washington DC, 1990
26. *Catholic Worker*, March-April 1993
27. *New Internationalist*, March 1992
28 Ruth Morris, Allan Nixon Lecture, Auckland, New Zealand, June 1994
29. *Harvard Law Journal*, Vol 107, 1994, pp2123-28
30. Robert F. Drinan, *National Catholic Reporter*, 9 September 1994
31. *Harvard Law Journal*, op cit
32. Ibid
33. *New Zealand Herald*, 11 April 1994
34. *The Press*, Christchurch, 22 August 1994
35. ACLU memo, 12 September 1993, in the *Congressional Quarterly*, 20 November 1993
36. *Sojourners*, 14 June 1990

SECTION TWO

Restorative Justice

Instead of defining justice as retribution, let us define justice as restoration.
If crime is injury, then justice will repair injuries and promote healing.

Howard Zehr

CHAPTER SIX

The Maori Restorative Tradition

An elderly Far North Maori has been banned from his home marae for a sex offence. A spokesman said the offender was a very active member on the marae, and was very embarrassed and humiliated by his actions. The six-month ban was a suitable penalty.

The case follows recent publicity about marae hearings in the Waikato that have resulted in seven Maori elders being stripped of their kaumatua status. The process, developed by the Hamilton child and protection agency Kokana Ngakau, has resulted in 18 cases of physical and sexual abuse being taken back to various marae.

Maori lore has a way of addressing Maori grievances, with court sessions being held on marae in accordance with tikana Maori, and whanau determining the sentence. Some court sessions had taken up to three days of non-stop discussion to resolve.

NZPA, September 1993

It will have come as a considerable surprise to most New Zealanders to learn that Maori have a traditional integrated system of criminal justice and that in some areas of Aotearoa to a degree it is still being used. The general perception among Pakeha is that such 'quaint customs' died out over a century ago.

Clearly this is not the case. Despite the strongest efforts of the 'one law for all' brigade, there obviously has been a parallel system of justice operating alongside the dominant English-derived system.

Modern Case Histories

Aroha Terry of Tainui, an expert in sexual abuse cases, claims marae justice is more effective than the traditional Pakeha justice system. In the latter, a person can be locked away for a few years in jail and no-one hears about it. They never have to face their accusers or take responsibility for their actions, and they never have to change. There is no healing for the victim, no healing for the whanau. In the Pakeha system there is no appropriate procedure for the whanau, and no empowerment for them to make decisions.

Under marae justice it is just the opposite. The purpose of marae justice is a healing for all: it is not a battleground. The process is primarily about hearing and helping the victim, healing the whanau, and helping and healing the perpetrator. It works for all three.

> Marae justice is set up to meet victims' needs. It is not about squashing the offender into the dirt. It is about recognising who got hurt – to hell with people saying society is the victim: it was *me*, not society, that got hurt.
>
> Marae justice takes the responsibility away from the victim and places it where it belongs – with the offender. It is particularly appropriate for dealing with sexual offences. The offender is the one who puts all the crap on the victim. We're so scared, we're so tidy in our little whares, in our lives, picking on the victim. It's all so wrong. I say go back to the offender and say 'Hey, this is your problem'.[1]

Waha Stirling of Ngai Tahu and Ngati Porou na Whanau Apanui, in speaking of his youthful days in the 1930s and 1940s on the East Coast, remembers that most cases of wrongdoing involving criminal behaviour were dealt with on the local marae by elders. Cases included all petty offending such as stealing and assault as well as more serious ones of sexual and child abuse. The police were only called in for more serious offending.

The process used was one of bringing the families together and talking it all through in a way that is very similar to the process now used in Aotearoa under the Children, Young Persons and Their Families Act.

The whanau of both sides in a complaint were invited to a hui. The accused needed to plead guilty and not hide what had been done. It was up to the accused's whanau to get to the root of the matter before the hearing began, and elicit a guilty plea if this was the case. In a sense the whole whanau was on trial so this usually wasn't hard to do. At the hui the elders would take the offender to task, with the kuia being particularly prominent in shaming the offender and the whole family. Often they were all reduced to tears.

Then, consultation between the parties would take place as to a suitable way of dealing with the matter, so as to heal any hurts and restore things to 'normal' again. Things stolen would have to be recovered or compensation paid. Damage would have to be repaired. The penalty usually also involved some compulsory work – sometimes offenders would be sent off to work on adjacent cattle stations if there was not enough work for them around the marae or village.

Waha's own uncle was accused of child abuse against a young girl. The charge of child abuse in those days often involved unacceptable levels of violence against youngsters through thrashings and hidings. A hui was held to which the Stirling family and that of the girl were invited. After the details were aired and the offences admitted, it was clear that both the uncle and the girl needed to be healed of the effects of what had taken place. The victim's taha wairua needed restoring; her shame as a victim needed to be overcome and returned.

The tohunga (priest) came and prayed special karakia for her restoration of spirit. Then regularly over a period of two or three months, the tohunga would go with her and her family to wash in the river – ritual washing to heal the spirit. This would be the process to bring her back from the darkness of whakama to the daylight, te marama.

The uncle was banished from the tribe and sent up north for two years, where he had to work out his punishment in the gumfields. At the same time he went through a process of anger management with an elder of the northern tribe and was forced to face some hard questions. Why did he abuse? How could he control it? Did he not appreciate the whare tangata, the sacred being of the person he abused? Why did he not respect women? What steps did he need to take to see the action was not repeated?

The northern chief took on the responsibility of overseeing the healing process. Eventually the offender was able to return home when this process was completed.

Hohua Tutengaehe of Ngai Te Rangi and Ngati Ranginui recalls a case when, as a 14-year-old boy in the late 1940s, he was asked to act as recorder in an attempted rape hearing. The attempt had got to a point where the assailant had allegedly removed the young woman's underwear before the assault ceased. The chief called a hui of the rangatira of each of the local marae. After whaikorero, the process began.

First the victim came in accompanied by her parents, her aunts and uncles, sisters and brothers and the whanau of the grandparents. Then the whanau of the assailant arrived. They sat on opposite sides of the meeting house.

The boy, who admitted to the offence, was about 17 years old, the girl a year younger. As soon as the boy pleaded guilty, a session of lectures started from the kuia, the old women present. They berated him for his behaviour, for the sacred tapu he had broken by attacking a young woman, for the shame he had brought on himself, his whanau, his people. In next to no time he and his family were reduced to tears.

Following that, the penalty was pronounced. It was decided that for the first 12 months, whenever there was a wedding or a tangi, the family of the boy had to supply all the meat and vegetables. In addition, he had to paint the meeting house. When they examined the meeting house they found that the weatherboards and roofing iron were decayed, so the family had to replace these.

After some time, because the meeting house belonged to them all, the girl and her whanau went along to help prepare the meals for the boy's family while they were working. The two sides came together in a gesture of reconciliation.

Eventually they all settled down and together repaired the dining-room and the surrounding fences. The whole process took about two years.

This was modern Maori justice in action – restorative, healing, reconciling. There were no names on the criminal pages of the media, no police record to haunt the boy in his future life, and the victim received due recognition in the process and was healed of her trauma.

It was a classic case from only a few decades ago where a serious offence was dealt with in a serious fashion through a restorative process rather than through the state court and prison system. The whole aim of the process was to restore the wellbeing of the victim and her whanau through imposing sanctions against the offender and his family. That the offence was treated seriously cannot be doubted, gauging from the time spent at the hui and the penalty – utu – exacted from the boy's family. They paid a high price in terms of whakama (shame), hours spent working, and money.

But marae justice is not just something from the past. In an *Inside New Zealand* television documentary, *Marae Justice*, shown in Aotearoa in August 1994, actual marae hearings were filmed and shown nationwide. These were examples employing a traditional Maori justice setting where the whanau acted as prosecutor and sentencing court.

We were taken to the Korapatu Marae where a 24-year-old local woman alleged she had been raped and sexually abused repeatedly between the ages of eight and 16 years. Three brothers were among her abusers. She described how she had been treated as a slave and raped repeatedly.

> It would happen once a day. Sometimes once a week. We thought it was normal. I can remember being dragged under the house. If I didn't go I got a hiding. I just let them do what they wanted. I was so terrified – I was really scared. I don't know why they hated me so much. I was just a little kid, trying to live, trying to survive.[2]

The three offending brothers had been summoned by the whanau to the hearing. Such is the power of the whanau that there is no escaping from them if they wish to remain a part of it. The family sit in judgment on the allegations; there were no lawyers, no judge, no police.

Aroha Terry, as advocate, read out the charges of multiple rape, sexual violation and abuse. All listened in silence. Each of the three men pleaded guilty. One added he was glad it had come out into the open. Another said he took full responsibility for what he had done. They all then listened to the woman speak of her pain, her abject suffering over many years, her feelings of rejection, distrust, hatred, anger. She finished by saying that after many months of counselling prior to the hearing, she now felt ready to forgive them. What had moved her finally to that point was hearing them acknowledge what they had done was wrong, that they took full personal responsibility for their actions, and that they deeply regretted the hurt and pain she had suffered.

The aroha present enabled healing and reconciliation to occur. The openness of the accused and their acceptance of responsibility coupled with a desire to change their behaviour and make some amends meant progress could be made towards healing for all.

The sentence for the three men as decided by the whanau was severe but positive. The whakama that each had experienced by appearing before other family members and their acceptance of responsibility and pleas of guilty were taken into consideration and given considerable weight.

Each was to undergo extensive counselling and commissioned to go to work on behalf of the whanau and tell others of the need to end sexual abuse. They had to speak to groups and families of their own experiences and offences, and encourage others to treat their children and their whanau with respect. This process was to be carefully monitored to make sure that there was full compliance.

The victim expressed delight at the progress made. She said she 'felt good' that the balance had been partially redressed and the men had acknowledged their offending. She was glad there were no more skeletons in the cupboard. Maori women generally found it hard to speak out, but she was glad that she had.[3]

Another woman featured in the same programme alleged abuse by her stepfather.

> I figured that if he abused me as the eldest, he might leave my sisters alone. I felt like I wanted to kill him. He used to hold me down over the wash-house sink with the broom handle. He told me he would kill me if I told Mum. I used to get into the shower and bath-tub and try and scrub myself clean.[4]

The stepfather pleaded guilty at a marae hearing. The whanau stripped him of his mana and matuatanga and kaumatua status and banned him from the marae. But eight months later when filming took place he was in denial. He claimed he was drunk all the time, and had never abused anyone.

There was a time when belonging to a gang almost certainly meant having to be involved with rape in order to be seen to be 'staunch'. Such was the case with Black Power, probably New Zealand's best-known gang. For years women were treated as objects to be enjoyed at gang members' behest, and no amount of imprisonment for rape and other charges of violence made any difference. Prison was seen as a place to recruit new members. The traditional retributive justice process could not stem the violence towards women. In effect it increased it.

Then came a dramatic shift in attitude. At their 1978 national convention, Black Power, led by their president, Rei Harris, banned rape. Rediscovery of traditional Maori justice and values had a significant part to play in this conversion. So too did the strength and integrity of the president and some of his chief supporters.

But for some old habits die hard. There were subsequent cases that Black Power dealt with themselves. Bill Maung, former judge and legal adviser to Black Power, tells how the gang dealt with such violations of their moral code.

He tells of one incident when a young woman came to the Wellington chapter and reported that she had been raped by three of their members. She preferred not to go to the police, so it was agreed they would be dealt with on a marae. Amster Reedy of Ngati Porou, at that time a lecturer at Teachers' College and a kaumatua, was one of about 50 who gathered to hear the case: Maori wardens, social workers, whanau, Black Power members.

After hearing the young woman's story, the hui reflected on what should happen to the three young men. One of them came from Taranaki and his kuia berated him tearfully, saying that their tribe had always walked with pride, and now he had made them all crawl seeking forgiveness. One suggestion was that they should all be exiled from Aotearoa forever, banished and forced to leave the country and the people they had so betrayed.

The offenders then took the floor and admitted the rapes. Their remorse was overwhelming, their desire to change and do reparation genuine. Pills and alcohol had obviously been contributing factors, though they claimed no mitigation from that source. They experienced tremendous shame in front of their whanau, their peers, their tribes. They vowed never to re-offend.

Then the young woman spoke, saying that she forgave them. Later, in explaining why, she said that for once in her life she had felt in control of a major situation, so she felt she could afford to be generous to them given the sorrow they had expressed.

Finally the penalty was spelt out. Quoting an old Maori proverb, Reedy noted that shame would be their principal punishment. There was, he said, no more powerful punishment in Maori society than whakama. People had been known to will themselves to death because the finger of shame had been pointed at them. The young men were also placed under close supervision and ordered to pay $20 a week each from their meagre incomes to the woman for six months. This constituted about a quarter of their incomes.

None of the men involved re-offended. One later committed suicide, though no definite connection was made with his rape offence. Another became a strong family man and a leader in the development of his whanau and people. Under Pakeha law, says Maung, they would still be sitting on all their anger in prison, while the woman, after a degrading court experience, would have become a marked woman and would have had to leave town.[5]

But is the marae justice outlined above a modern version of traditional Maori justice, or one culturally influenced by Pakeha traditions?

Moana Jackson of Ngati Porou and Ngati Kahungunu says that research shows that this type of marae justice is a product of the Crown which, early this century, set up marae or Maori Committees under Maori Council legislation. They were set up not to respect the articles of the Treaty of Waitangi, but to destroy Maori social and judicial structures. A specific purpose of the legislation was to break down surviving iwi and hapu authority by replacing them with Crown-funded bodies.

He says that these committees practising 'marae justice' had very limited authority and very limited subordinate jurisdiction to 'hear' cases on a marae. The structures formed part of the subordination of Maori decision-making to one Pakeha law. He believes its use today confirms that subordination.[6]

The Traditional Approach

The cases outlined above would not then have come as any surprise to those who know Maori well and are acquainted with their traditional concepts of justice and law. Such law was recognised by the early colonial settlers.

Edward Shortland, Protector of Aborigines, writing in 1856, described his understanding of Maori law. He said Maori sought compensation rather than punishment for the injury or crime. He complained that their methods of redress were often unjust in his opinion, 'with innocent persons being made to suffer for the faults of others'. For instance, in cases of adultery, the relations of the guilty parties were liable to suffer, and sometimes even the relations of the injured husband.[7]

He saw the question of honour and satisfaction as a major component of Maori understanding of justice. He wrote that the friendly involvement of a stranger in their quarrels was never taken amiss by Maori and it often enabled a peaceful settlement by helping the weaker party save face and withdraw. He noted that Maori always sought to take their stand and make a point, even if eventually they conceded the argument.[8]

Criminologist John Pratt confirms the restorative nature of the process. He writes that the purpose of the justice system, which usually took the form of a hearing on the marae (area in front of the meeting house or wharenui) or inside a special meeting house called a wharerunanga, was to investigate the matter and try to restore the balance that had been disturbed. This usually meant redressing the harm done to the victim.

The quantity of redress would depend on the degree of the offence: a form of compensation (utu) for some, with mediation to remove causes of tension. Other offences – say some breaches of tapu – would be seen to be so serious that death would be demanded. Whatever, the interests of the victim and his or her family or tribe were central to the administration of justice. Indeed, the victim's 'right' to justice could be handed down from one generation to another and could be pursued against the wrongdoer and his next of kin or tribe. Hence the importance attached to dispute proceedings, which might last for days while a resolution was being negotiated.

Pratt says that here, as well, the justice system did not exist in isolation from the rest of society (as with the elitism and professional dominance to be found in the European model) but was completely integrated within it, rooted in the everyday experiences of Maori people. The most prevalent sanction seems to have been utu – and the usual method of securing satisfaction in this way would be for the offended party and his kinsmen to act as a raiding party (taua muru) and plunder the offender and his kin. The scope and extent of the raid would have been agreed in advance.[9]

Shortland presented a 19th-century Pakeha version of how Pakeha generally viewed Maori behaviour. He wrote that thieving was not regarded as disgraceful, and was therefore a common vice of the youth of the country . However, when a thief was detected, he was not allowed to escape without punishment. Once, when Shortland was absent, his house at Maketu was broken into by two young men, who stole some small items. They were soon discovered, and most of the property was restored. Afterwards a public meeting was called to deal with the matter. It so happened that one of them was the son of a chief, who owned a piece of land near his house. Shortland had wished to include the land within his boundary. The owner refused to part with it, as the soil was rich and the situation convenient for a garden. Now he offered it voluntarily as compensation for the theft.[10]

Another major component of Maori law was muru, which in essence amounted to compensation. It was enforced by a raiding or stripping party. A person may have been guilty of some offence or may have suffered an accident. In either event muru was appropriate. While Europeans dreaded the arrival of the stripping party – the taua muru – the Maori would welcome it. For them it would be a point of honour to have food ready for the stripping party on their arrival. Their social position would be enhanced, not diminished, by the rigour of the stripping.[11]

Not every tribe followed the same pattern nor employed the same sanctions. Teone Taare Tikao, a leading chief of Ngai Tahu at the turn of the century, explained his tribe's approach to muru.

> Muru was not common in some parts of the South Island, but we had it in Banks Peninsula. Tapui, a son of Whiua, was taken prisoner by Te Rauparaha to the North Island, where he married a Ngati-Awa woman. They came to Akaroa at the time of the rongopai (when peace was made and Christianity came in). He died and a North Island man of Akaroa took her to wife. She was a putao (widow), and this was not according to custom, so the relatives felt they must muru him

and kill someone else. So the people went to plunder him but there was not much to take. The woman died soon after. In the old days the muru party would have taken the goods and burnt the house, but they did not go so far [this time].[12]

Differing Features

The fundamental differences between Maori and Pakeha law were many and varied. The whole English system of courts with prosecutors, judges and lawyers skilfully weaving their way through legal precedents and volumes of law and acts of Parliament was totally alien to Maori. So too was the notion that the English law dealt only with the individuals involved. Maori law always presumed a collective or corporate responsibility for offending and restoration while Pakeha law looked only at the individual and his or her guilt.

The Maori concept was built on the most fundamental of all Maori values – that we are all part of one another. The Pakeha concept was built on the notion that each person is individually responsible for his or her own plight. Maori found imprisonment abhorrent, whereas Pakeha took it to be the norm.

In two areas in particular was there a fundamental difference in terms of redress. Utu, or compensation and satisfaction, was an important concept at the very heart of Maori justice. It found no comparable expression in English law. And muru, a formalised concept of retributive compensation, was a feature central to Maori but alien to English law.

In ancient times not all cases ended up in complete reconciliation. Maori justice provided the death penalty or banishment from the tribe as appropriate sanctions on occasions. But the aim was always restorative: restore the mana of the tribe and of the offended parties. If the victims were of high birth, then sometimes only drastic measures such as death could achieve this. While execution may appear to be harsh to modern eyes, it should be noted that at this point in history, England had more than 200 offences that warranted execution, and a further quota that resulted in transportation to the colonies as convicts.

Harry Evison, noted historian of the Ngai Tahu people, comments on this point in his history of the tribe. He says that being fettered in floating dungeons for hard labour across the Atlantic was not for Africans alone. Since the year 1620 British convicts had also been transported as forced labour to the American colonies. There they had to work as virtual slaves on the estates of wealthy planters, under a strict discipline enforced by flogging.

In 1717 the British Parliament prescribed seven years' transportation for minor offences of dishonesty and 14 years for men reprieved from hanging. In Captain Cook's time about 600 British convicts were sent to America each year, mostly for theft. Transportation and hanging were the normal punishments prescribed by British law for theft or forgery. The enforcement of the law protecting private property was strict, and (as in Te Wai Pounamu) those who broke the rules met with violent punishment. Times were hard, and the poor were desperate. But the British authorities were just as desperate to rid the country of its 'criminal class'. Hundreds were hanged in public each year, attracting large crowds of spectators. The corpses were left rotting in chains.[13]

Hohua Tutengaehe recalls hearing from his mother that the brother of the Ariki, a very high chief, had raped a woman of high birth. The hearing was held at a hui on the marae and it was the unanimous decision of the rangatira present that he would have to pay with his life for assaulting the tapu of the tangata. He was executed publicly on the marae by his older brother, the Ariki, so that 'the stain and blemish was removed from the aristocracy of ancient bloodlines'. He was clubbed in the temple. Before the execution, the brothers clasped each other in tears, with the doomed man's last words to his brother being 'Kei te pai (it's all right)'.

Not all murderers were executed. Shortland recorded the case in 1844 of Hinekina, of the Hapu Katahuriri. She lived at Moeraki with a Pakeha by whom she had two children, plus a child of about 12 years old by a former husband. The child went missing unexpectedly and the mother was unable to explain its absence, so Te Ruakaio, a near relative of Tuhawaiki, and two other women went searching. They eventually found the child's body in a waterhole and some whalers from the settlement helped them retrieve it. When confronted with the dead child, Hinekina confessed to the killing.

> The natives generally, as well as the Europeans, were very indignant. Hinekino subsequently fled to Waitaki, but has been brought back by the European who lived with her, with whom she still remains.[14]

After the Treaty

The settler government was in no mood to allow such a widely divergent system of justice to exist parallel to its own imported British system. Yet the Treaty of Waitangi clearly stated that Maori laws and customs were to be maintained. Maori law and the process of Maori justice have an inherent validity as taonga (treasures) and as an expression of rangatiratanga (authority) guaranteed in article 2 of the treaty document.

As Moana Jackson said in a recent submission to Parliament:

> Under article 1 of the Maori version, the Maori gave kawanatanga to the Queen. To the Maori this term meant simply that the Queen should provide for the good order and security of the country by exercising control over the Pakeha settlers, while recognising the special rights which accompanied the tangata whenua status of Maori. Recognition of these rights carried with it an acknowledgment of the laws and institutions existing within Maori society. To ensure their

maintenance within a rapidly changing world, the Maori saw those laws as operating in a parallel system to that of the Crown.[15]

Pakeha clearly saw it differently, and to them kawanatanga corresponded to a more absolute concession of sovereignty, resulting ultimately in the supremacy of the Pakeha way. Jackson again:

> The undertaking to preserve 'other properties' in article 2 was translated to include 'all things highly prized such as their own customs and culture'. However, although Maori law was frequently described as a 'quaint custom', it has never been regarded as sufficiently quaint to be protected under article 2. Neither has there been an acceptance of the Maori belief that the 'tino rangatiratanga' guaranteed over those customs was an assertion of authority and control. Any recognition of Maori law, Maori authority and Maori participation in general law-making processes was excluded. In effect, this has been used to deny Maori involvement in, and thus excluded Maori values from, the law-making process.

Article 2 of the Maori version of the treaty guarantees the right of rangatiratanga over taonga or prized things. In article 4 the treaty ensures protection of 'te ritenga Maori', that is, the basic threads of law, religion, language and other taonga that wove Maori society together. Those articles in conjunction recognise the general authority of Maori people to monitor the conduct of their own.[16]

In other words, Maori were guaranteed that their system of law would be protected and allowed to develop under the terms of the treaty. That they have not be thus allowed is clearly evident. The law of Aotearoa has been consistently in breach of the Treaty of Waitangi virtually since its signing.

What were the particular ideals and institutions of Maori law at the time? Did they contain a clearcut code of behaviour and how widely was it accepted?

Jackson, in his parliamentary submission, argued that such a code clearly existed. The system was clear and defined, and Maori people knew which acts were unacceptable – hara or crimes. The definition of hara rose from a framework of social relationships based on group rather than individual concerns. The rights of individuals, or the hurts they may suffer when their rights were abused, were indivisible from the welfare of the whanau, the hapu, the iwi. Each had reciprocal obligations found in a shared genealogy, and a set of behavioural precedents established by common tipuna.

> Those precedents became *te tikanga o nga hara* (the criminal code) and were accepted as binding because they 'were the law that came from the wisdom of our past ... which binds us to our tipuna'. They became part of the process by which certain acts were made subject to sanction. These definitions of unacceptability were based not so much on the fact that people had individual rights, but rather that they had collective responsibilities. They were based too

on the specific belief that all people had an inherent tapu that must not be abused, and on the general perception that society could only function if all things, physical and spiritual, were held in balance.

Jackson goes on to explain that the commission of nga hara would damage that tapu and upset that balance. Constraints on behaviour, a criminal law, had to be developed to preserve harmony within and among individuals and their community. That law was not an isolated set of rules to be invoked only upon an infringement of accepted behavioural limits. Neither was it part of a distinct discipline to be 'learned' separately from the spiritual and religious beliefs of society.

Instead, it grew out of and was inextricably woven into the religious and hence the everyday framework of Maori life. It reflected a special significance that was manifest in the spiritual ties of the people to their Gods, and the whakapapa shared between individuals and the ancestors who bore them. The Maori lived not under the law but with it. This inter-relationship affected the definition of the criminal act itself, the ideas of responsibility for it, and the process by which the hara would be redressed.

Jackson says that because individuals were inextricably linked by whakapapa to their whanau and iwi, so were their actions the unavoidable responsibility of the wider group. An offender could not be isolated as solely responsible for wrongdoing; a victim could never be isolated as bearing alone the pain of an offence. There was a collective rather than an individual criminal responsibility, a sense of indirect as well as direct liability.[17]

As in indigenous cultures the world over, the inter-relationship between the deities, the ancestors and the living thus provided the base of definition of both crimes and responsibility. Certain acts were criminal not so much because of the immediate imbalance they caused or the social dysfunction they created, but because of the behavioural prescriptions laid down through the interdependence of the living and the ancestors. The act itself was less important in explaining offending than the reasons why it was defined as unacceptable.

John Pratt says the act of rape was thus a hara punishable by death, not just because it physically hurt the victim, or because, as in early English law, it damaged a chattel owned by a man. Rather it was forbidden because it violated the inherent tapu of women. It thus in turn upset the spiritual, emotional and physical balance within the victim herself, and within the relationships she had within her community and tipuna. The act of rape was therefore proscribed to protect that balance and to preserve her tapu. The crime of incest was similarly predicated in a specific weave of ancestral and spiritual prohibition.[18]

Jackson says that in this sense, Maori law was no different from the laws of other indigenous peoples. The purpose of the legal process was to ensure order and the survival of the collective and the individual. The nature of what was to survive, what was to be ordered, was an intricately interwoven taniko centring on group relationships, and the respect and reverence for tipuna and land from which the sense of order came. The law thus embodied ideals, hopes and potential, as well as a longing for harmony. It strengthened and directed individuals and iwi. The nexus between the spiritual and the temporal was so close as to refuse separation. The links between culture and matauranga were so close as to be indivisible in the process of defining wrongdoing.[19]

It is clear, Jackson says, that in pre-colonial times there were specially trained tohunga or experts in the law who chaired or supervised hearings. It was not just the kaumatua who sat in judgment – the hearings included experts in law and Maori legal processes.

There were educated and trained tohunga who dealt with legal matters in concert with representatives of the disputant whanau. These representatives were often pakeke, but the process could not function without those trained to administer it.[20]

He says that if Maori are to reclaim their own judicial authority then it will not be as some 'informal' process that anybody can call or set up. Its principal aim will be that of mea tuhonohono, a process designed to ensure ongoing 'bringing together' or harmony. It will be a process involving all parties, mediated by appropriate tohunga, backed by the authority to impose sanction, and implemented to seek the restoration of balance.[21]

One System, Not Two

The prevailing belief among 19th-century government officials and settlers was that the British system was the best in the world. They never really sought to understand the different goals and processes of Maori justice. The Treaty of Waitangi was soon forgotten.

The British government was not keen to allow two parallel systems – one retributive, one primarily restorative – to develop in its new colony. Pratt explains that in the last century, the British Colonial Office and New Zealand governments pursued a policy of assimilation toward Maori people in regard to their modes of punishment and dispute resolution.

Although Maori were formally made citizens of New Zealand under the terms of the Treaty of Waitangi in 1840, the concept of citizenship was seen as having much wider meaning than this. It referred to the various modes of behaviour, practices, social codes and institutions that together represented 'the British way of life' in the 19th century. The assimilation process referred to the methods by which Maori people gradually achieved this status and in return for which had to give up their land, culture and institutions, including the power to punish in their own way. They were expected to stop being Maori and, instead, to act and behave as Europeans.

This is not to say that Maoridom itself was dismantled, to disappear forever. What it did mean was that Maori were ultimately forced outside of and excluded from official power and administration. Any subsequent assertion of it would take the form of resistance to European citizenship and the British way of life, on which official power had come to be based.[22]

The New Zealand government was hell-bent on a process of assimilation, meaning that traditional Maori customs that in any way affected European settlers had to be removed. Within months of the signing of the treaty, Governor Hobson reflected the views of the settlers when he sought to impose the British legal system upon Maori and Pakeha alike. Hobson believed Maori habits to be so different to those of civilised life, and their practices so repugnant to the customs of Englishmen, that he scarcely hoped to preserve peace when the settlers became more numerous. He also looked to the simple assertion of his authority, rather than some system of practical co-operation with the chiefs, as the solution to New Zealand's difficulties.[23]

Maori culture, traditions and values were not to be allowed to develop alongside those of the Pakeha society if there was any way they would undermine the ideology, identity and power of the new government. Pratt confirms that the form of colonisation and legal protection envisaged by Glenelg (Secretary of State to the Colonies based in London) assumed that assimilation of the Maori into 'the British way of life' would be the result and that they would become British citizens in the widest meaning of the term.[24]

Thus the decimation of the traditional restorative philosophy of Maori justice was set in place by British officials in London, many of whom never set foot on New Zealand soil.

There were some in New Zealand who tried to modify English law to accommodate some aspects of traditional law. In 1844, under Governor Fitzroy, the Native Protectorate Department proposed the establishment of Native Courts, which would be administered by the Protector and local chiefs. Mixed juries would be used for serious cases. As Pratt notes, judgments would be recorded in the manner of British practice, and thereby establish judicial precedence and certainty. Meanwhile the presence of the chiefs would give the proceedings added authority. It was hoped the practice of muru would fall into disuse.

In cases other than rape and murder, a Maori would be allowed to go free on payment of a £20 deposit. In cases of theft, Maori offenders could escape imprisonment by paying four times the value of the goods stolen – recognition of the utu principle – and utu could also be enacted by Maori complainants against Pakeha defendants. In addition, 'people of the native race were not liable for imprisonment for debt'. The principle was extended in the Fines for Assaults Ordinance 1845: the court was given the power to award compensation from the fine imposed provided that the sum so awarded did not amount to more than half the fine levied.[25]

Fitzroy's policies were very much out of step with the wishes and views of the European settlers. For them, the misguided philanthropy of the Colonial Office was actually preventing the advancement of civilisation. In their eyes, formally recognising the indigenous punishment process would only help prolong Maori culture. It could only be harmful for the 'natives' as well as hindering their own plans for settlement.

Alan Ward gives credit to Fitzroy's effort to include restorative dimensions in the law, saying it was a genuine attempt to make English law more acceptable to the Maori by incorporating a useful point of custom (utu).[26]

The rejection by London of Fitzroy's Native Exemption Ordinance was to have far-reaching consequences for race relations and the administration of justice in New Zealand. The effects are still with us. Fitzroy's successor, Governor Grey, was instructed by London to amend the ordinance to allow British law to assume undoubted supremacy.

In 1846 Grey moved to systematically undermine the traditional authority of chiefs by appointing magistrates who would have summary jurisdiction over everyone, Maori and Pakeha. This was a major first step to total dominance of the legal processes by English law.

Some elements of Maori law did prevail for some years afterwards. The Native District Regulations Act 1858 specified that Maori, through local runanga rather than chiefs, could dispense justice in minor matters. These matters included drunkenness and the control of dogs.

A ministerial memorandum of 1861 outlined the government's intentions. Here the government was speaking with a forked tongue, for while it did empower local runanga in minor matters, it further disempowered Maori by refusing to allow dimensions with no place in English law to be used. These included such things as breeches of tapu, and making taua muru on the innocent relatives of offenders. This latter process was part of the notion of collective responsibility. Even so, restoration rather than retribution remained at the heart of runanga justice.

Governor Grey in 1862 clarified the position of runanga further. Now, as 'new institutions', there would be village runanga (composed of elected villagers) under the auspices of new officers called civil commissioners. Grey explained that his policy through the runanga would propose local laws concerning cattle pounds, fences, branding cattle, thistles and weeds, dogs, spirits and drunkenness, putting down bad customs of the old Maori law such as the taua muru, and the various things that especially concerned the people living in the district. They would also make regulations about schools, roads (if they wished for them) and other matters which that promote the public good of that district.[27]

In effect, the runanga seem to function in ways not too dissimilar to the subsequent development of borough and county councils. Regular use of runanga for the purposes the colonial government intended failed to materialise as bigger issues such as the struggle over land assumed prominence.

In modern times there have been various attempts by Maori to assume limited control over their judicial affairs. Ranginui Walker has outlined four cases of a restorative process among Maori enacted on urban marae in one suburb between 1967-69.

One case involved a woman accused of child neglect, holding noisy drinking parties for under-age youth, and harbouring a runaway state ward. She appeared before a local Maori committee to answer the allegations. After whaikorero the purpose of the hearing was outlined. After hearing evidence the court dismissed the first two allegations and found her guilty on the harbouring charge. As penalty, she was warned off the consumption of liquor for 12 months, ordered to seek budgeting advice, and severely reprimanded by her elders.

In another case a woman was accused of neglecting her four children. She had failed to respond to warnings. As a disciplinary measure, the Maori court sent a working party of local people to her home to help her clean up the house and get her back on her feet.

In the third case, four young boys were accused of wilfully chopping down public trees. The parents were called to court and ordered to buy young trees and replant the area their sons had devastated. And in the fourth case, a Pakeha lodged a complaint against his Maori neighbour of having incessant noisy late-night parties and of using bad language and verbal abuse. The defendant was severely reprimanded and fined.

At the end of the case the accused had to accept the findings of the committee. Healing and forgiveness were seen as a necessary part of the process.[28]

Conclusion

There have been many other modern examples of local Maori committees dealing with offenders accused of various types of criminal activity, ranging from stealing to rape. The cases of the kaumatua in the Far North in September 1993 and those of other Waikato kaumatua stripped of their status by marae justice indicate that the parallel process continues. Hohua Tutengaehe speaks of many other such instances right up until the present time. Acts of stealing and assault were the most common, and there are many instances where police action was prevented because the local Maori people dealt with the offenders themselves in the traditional Maori way.

There have been many occasions where gang criminal violations of the law have been dealt with on this basis. Not once has anyone been let off lightly in terms of sanction. Often the penalty has seemed to be more severe than that which a state court might hand down. But the aim of the process is the same as it was for centuries before the immigrants arrived: to respond appropriately to the violation of law in a manner that allows full restoration of all parties to good relationships within their families, and allows for the healing of the hurt experienced by the whanau, the hapu and the tribe.

Footnotes

1. *Inside New Zealand* documentary *Marae Justice*, TV3, August 1994
2. Ibid
3. Ibid
4. Ibid
5. Pamela Stirling, *NZ Listener*, 14 May 1990
6. Letter, Moana Jackson to the author, 17 October 1994
7. Edward Shortland, *Traditions and Superstitions of the New Zealanders*, Longman, Brown, Green, Longman and Roberts, London, 1856. Reprint by Capper Press, Christchurch, 1980, p236
8. Ibid, p238
9. John Pratt, *Punishment in a Perfect Society, The New Zealand Penal System 1840-1939*, Victoria University Press, 1992, p35
10. Shortland, op cit, p240
11. O. Wilson, *From Hongi Hika to Hone Heke*, John McIndoe Ltd, Dunedin, 1985, p127
12. *Tikao Talks*, told by Teone Taare Tikau to Herries Beattie, Penguin, 1990, pp153-54
13. Harry C. Evison, *Te Wai Pounamu*, Aoraki Press, Christchurch, 1993, p22
14. Shortland, letter to Fitzroy, 1844, Papers Relative to New Zealand, No. 71. Also found in *The Southern Districts of New Zealand by Edward Shortland*, 1851, reprinted by Capper Press, Christchurch, 1974, pp132-33
15. Moana Jackson, 'Criminality and the Exclusion of Maori', from *Essays on Criminal Law in New Zealand – Towards Reform*, edited by Neil Cameron and Simon France, Victoria University Press, Wellington, 1990, p32
16. Ibid, p33
17. Ibid, p30
18. Platt, op cit, p13
19. Jackson, op cit, pp27-28
20. Moana Jackson, paper 'A Maori Justice System', Maori Law Society Annual Hui, Te Herenga Marae, 26 August 1994
21. Letter, Moana Jackson to the author, 17 October 1994
22. Platt, op cit, p13
23. Alan Ward, *A Show of Justice*, Auckland University Press, Oxford University Press, 1973, p58
24. Platt, op cit, p32
25. Ibid, p42
26. Ward, op cit, p67
27. Platt, op cit, p53
28. Ranginui Walker, 'The Politics of Voluntary Association', from *Conflict and Compromise*, edited by I.H. Kawharu, 1975, A.H. and A.W. Reed, Wellington, pp175-78

CHAPTER SEVEN

A Gift to the World:
Youth Justice in Aotearoa

Children's Court, July 1964:

Three youths, each aged 16, appeared today for sentence on six charges of car conversion. Stephen Menzies, Jason Pirihio, and Robert Pound had pleaded guilty to the charges. They said that they were bored and just having fun. They had not damaged the cars. All the offending had taken place on the night preceding Otago's challenge for the Ranfurly Shield.

The magistrate, Mr Raymond Brown SM, said that the community was fed up to the back teeth with young hooligans stealing as they wished, and joy-riding around town. He said that he planned to put a stop to such anti-social behaviour before it got out of hand. He added that he hoped the effect of his sentence would deter other young people from following in the defendants' footsteps. He sentenced each defendant to borstal training. This is a variable sentence ranging from four months to two years to be served at Invercargill Borstal.

Social Welfare report, July 1994:

A youth aged 16 who admitted stealing a total of six cars over a 12-hour period on a recent Friday night met with representatives of his family, the police, the Department of Social Welfare and four of the car owners in a family group conference convened by Ms Cecily Hamara. After opening with karakia, the kaumatua of the family spoken of his embarrassment that one of his nephews had got himself into so much trouble.

Constable Bernice McGara, from the Youth Aid section of the police, read out the summary of facts. This included the information that one of the cars had a front fender damaged and another had interior damage. The young man then admitted the offences, saying he had been 'out of it' on drugs at the time. One car owner angrily said that didn't help him get to an important meeting on time and he had ended up paying $56 for a taxi. Another said he had appreciated the youth's guilty pleas but wondered whether or not the whole episode not might be repeated once this case was over. A third said that he had lost his $200 no-claim bonus claim from the insurance company and wondered how the youth felt about that.

The co-ordinator said it was up to the group to arrive at a suitable penalty. After further discussion among family members, who spoke of their experience of the youth, his inability to make friends and his waywardness at school, the family retired to discuss what they thought an appropriate penalty might be. After a cup of tea the conference reconvened and the family put forward their proposal. They suggested that the youth repay both the money for the no-claim bonus and the taxi fee. Further to that, he agreed to see a counsellor with a view to entering the Odyssey House drug programme.

He accepted the offer of one of the car owners to be taught to drive properly and eventually get a licence. In exchange he agreed to cut that owner's lawns each Saturday during the following summer. All present agreed on this procedure.

Right now a revolution is occurring in the field of youth justice in Aotearoa. A new paradigm of justice is operating, which is very traditional in its philosophy, yet revolutionary in its effects. A restorative philosophy of justice has replaced a retributive one. Ironically, 150 years after the traditional Maori restorative praxis was abolished in Aotearoa, youth justice policy is once again operating from the same philosophy.

With the introduction of the Children, Young Persons and Their Families Act in 1989, the Labour government initiated the most sweeping reform of juvenile justice our country has seen this century. In fact it appears as a new concept, and in many parts of the world its implementation in New Zealand is being watched with increasing envy.

No longer are young offenders immediately arrested, charged and taken before the Children's or Young Offenders' Court and dealt with like adult offenders. In the vast majority of cases, after they have been apprehended by the police they are restored to their families and with considerable speed a new less formal process gets under way.

Its aim is to restore the wellbeing of the community by having the offenders face up to their responsibility for their crime. Victims, who are normally shut out of the process, are offered an opportunity of being involved in the follow-up. As Australian criminologist John Braithwaite points out, this reforming has the effect of bringing shame and personal and family accountability for wrongdoing back into the justice process.[1]

Judge F. W. M. McElrea, Youth Court liaison judge for Auckland, suggests that there are three radical changes involved in this new process. They involve the transfer of power from the state to the community, the use of the family group conference as the mechanism for producing a negotiated community response, and the involvement of victims as key participants, making possible a healing process for victim, offender and the community.

In the old model of justice the judge is in control, representing the state and exercising authority given by the state either to impose punishment or to direct intervention in peoples' lives for 'welfare' reasons. By contrast, in the new model the principle task of the judge is to facilitate and encourage the implementation of solutions devised through the group family conference procedure, and to act as a backup if these solutions are not implemented.[2]

Judge Michael Brown, principal Youth Court judge for New Zealand, asks judges to aid this process by asking who is the community? What are its strengths? How are those strengths best made use of? He notes that the concept of a judge trying to facilitate the strengths of others and bring them to the fore is radically different to the controlling position of the traditional judge.

At the heart of the revolution in youth justice in Aotearoa is the transfer of power from the state to the family group conference. In the traditional court, the key players are the judge, the prosecutor, the defence lawyer and the offenders. With the family group conference the key players are the offender, his or her family, the victim and their support group, with the facilitate, the police and other professionals all present in 'helping roles'. They assist the process so that the offender, within his 'family group' – which may or may not include only his immediate birth family – is helped to recognise the damage done and can be confronted by the victim as to the negative effects being experienced. Often victims have become more nervous, less trusting and retain considerable anger about the offence.

A key player in the family group conference is the victim. This represents a radical departure from the retributive system still prevalent in our adult system. The victim is encouraged to join the conference, express feelings about the offences, and then be part of the discussion of what might be a suitable sanction for the offender. This is acknowledged as usually being a very healing process for most victims, provided they are given adequate time and opportunity to be properly involved.

The Process

It is the role of the Youth Justice Co-ordinator to convene the family group conference, with the help of social workers. Generally the offender's family nominate the venue, which can vary. Sometimes their own homes are best suited, sometimes a church hall, a friend's home, a marae. Sometimes even a police cell has been used, though this is not usually considered to be appropriate.

Often the proceedings are opened by the offender's family. Many start with karakia or prayer. What happens next is worked out by the participants: there is no set formal procedure. Often the co-ordinator, after introducing people, will have the police summary of facts read. This can be challenged by the offender and may be amended on the spot. The offender then is usually invited to respond. If the offender denies the allegations, the conference is adjourned to enable a Youth Court hearing to be held. In the vast majority of cases the offender admits guilt, sometimes offering an explanation as to why he offended.

Then the victim is invited to respond. This can take a variety of forms. A fleshing-out of how the incident has affected the wellbeing of the victim will usually follow. For example, if a burglary has been admitted, it may emerge that the property stolen had belonged to a grandmother and had sentimental value, that the ring taken was perhaps a dead mother's wedding ring, that the clothing stolen was to have been worn at a wedding, that the tools taken were work tools and irreplaceable.

Sometimes women express their feelings that in invading their home, a burglar has invaded their very privacy. Some describe this feeling as being akin to sexual violation. The offender may find out that the victim now cannot sleep at night, is scared of the dark, or has withdrawn from community groups because of mistrust of strangers.

This will usually all come as a complete shock to offenders, who thought they were only pinching a few things to trade for drugs. Deborah Hollings, a lawyer with wide experience in youth justice, says it never appears in the summary of facts, and very rarely in the victim impact reports, that this was not just a car being stolen. This offence wrecked a very important part of the victim's life.

That sense of meeting eyeball to eyeball is a very important aspect of the family group conference (FGC). It means the young person cannot remain aloof; he has to be confronted by his victim. It is also a chance from the victim's viewpoint to get his anger out, a chance to state the repercussions, and a chance to reach across communities. Often there is a racial aspect there as well.

Hollings says there is also the process of the victim actually being reaffirmed, because the last time he saw his offender may have been in a dark alleyway. This time he is seeing his offender surrounded by his family, who are frequently crying with shame. In some 50 percent of cases (Hollings' guess) the offender is also crying with shame. The victim is re-empowered by that process.[3]

Usually there follows an apology. The highly charged atmosphere, the tearful response of many, often means the offender is overcome with remorse at realising the damage caused. At this point the real healing begins because, to use a term coined by Judge McElrea, 'responsible reconciliation' begins.

Then the penalty is discussed. All have a voice as to what is appropriate. The victim's views are again obtained at that point. Usually they are interested mostly in putting the wrong right, in reparation, in an apology, in having the young person come and work for them or a member of their family. Sometimes that conflicts, interestingly enough, with the police view.

So the victim is very powerful, they have a power of veto, as does everyone else in the FGC. The police then give their views as to what they would see as appropriate. The co-ordinators state the type of penalties they would see as appropriate for the type of offence and what funding is available from the department.

At that stage the family group retires on its own. Then the FGC comes back together, reunited, and the family spokesperson stands up and announces what the family has resolved in terms of penalty. There are sometimes further negotiations if the police or the victim are not happy, but usually there is agreement.

The meeting will then generally wind up with everyone having the chance to say how they feel about the process and sharing any other thoughts. Usually that ends with everyone saying that they wish the best of luck to the young person. Most cases end on that very positive note. Then the family close the meeting in a way appropriate to them.[4]

Research conducted by Dr Gabrielle Maxwell, senior research officer for the Commission for Children, and Dr Allison Morris of the Institute of Criminology, Cambridge, shows that the FGC does not always follow this rather idyllic process. In research covering the first three years of the process, in an average of 42 percent of cases the professionals did not leave the families alone to discuss a proposed penalty. In one area of the country this was 63 percent – nearly two-thirds of the cases.[5]

Sadly too in most cases the background to the offending was not discussed at any length. An exploration of the factors leading to the offending was either rare or made in random or haphazard fashion. Alcohol or drug use, for example, was raised and discussed for only some of the young people whose pattern of offending seemed to involve substance abuse.[6]

Despite some of these initial hiccups, this is clearly an exciting development in the field of criminal justice in Aotearoa. In effect the state has been removed from the centre of the justice equation and replaced by those most affected: the offender, the victim, and their families, who make up the community. For the victims there is a special place. While all their scars may not be healed initially and while full satisfaction may not be achieved, at the very least they are invited into the heart of the process.

As criminologist John Braithwaite says, sometimes moving gestures of healing come from the victim side. They waive their right to compensation from an unemployed young offender who cannot afford it. They invite them to their home for dinner a week after the conference. They help to find an unemployed young offender a job, a homeless young person a home. In one amazing case, a female victim who had been robbed by a young offender at the point of a gun had the offender live in her home as part of the agreed plan of action.

People can be amazing when they are enmeshed in institutions that invite them to care about each other instead of hate each other. The surprising thing is that victims, who so often call for more blood in traditional Western justice systems, in New Zealand frequently plead with the police to waive punishment and 'give the kid another chance'. Partly this happens because victims get an insight through the process of dialogue into the shocking life circumstances the young offender has had to confront.[7]

Given the weaknesses inherent in human nature and the scarred backgrounds of many offenders and victims, it is remarkable what can be achieved. Often it takes a group consciousness to shake the bravado and macho attitude and allow something of the pain of the victim to penetrate the tough exterior.

Braithwaite points out that young offenders use a variety of techniques to protect themselves from the shame of what they have done. This collective encounter with the harm done is the best chance for piercing the barriers young offenders have erected. Quite often the anger or grief of the victim will miss its mark, going straight over the head of a young offender, on whom it has no emotional impact. But the grief of the victim might pierce the heart of the offender's mother as she sits behind him. Then it can be her sobbing that rips away the armour that protects the offender's emotions.

In short, the strength of the New Zealand process is that it is neither individualistic or dyadic (as in traditional US victim-offender mediation) but that it engages multiplex communities of concern. Emotions of shame and feelings of responsibility are often brought out because shafts of emotion bounce from person to person within the room in unpredictable ways. When collectivities as well as individuals are targets of shaming, it is harder for responsible individuals to shrug off the shame.[8]

The ideal would be full reconciliation and healing, and it will happen in some instances. In most, particularly where there is personal injury involved, it probably won't. But at least in putting a human face on the crime it opens up the healing process. And that has to be good for everyone.

Background to Change

The Children, Young Persons and Their Families Act only came into existence in 1989. It was born out of the frustration of many in the juvenile justice field who found that the philosophy underpinning the former system left two major negative effects. The first was an orientation towards more offending, the second was the encouragement towards dependency on welfare as a way of life.

Previously youth offenders had often ended up in child welfare residential homes or, after serious offences, in detention centres (youth prisons), corrective training institutions or borstal. Here they were placed in state custody with other youthful offenders from similarly deprived backgrounds. For many such institutions provided their first real bonding with peers. For others, a real identity developed with a 'bad boy/bad girl' image that could only lead to lives as adult criminals. For all, new anti-social behaviour patterns were developed, along with new criminal skills.

The end result for too many was that such residential institutions became the first step along the road of habitual criminal behaviour and a lifetime in and out of jails. Prison chaplains and others well remember observing numerous reunions as new inmates arrived in prison and were reunited with old friends from one or other of the state's many residential homes.

Michael Doolan, Southern Regional Manager of the New Zealand Children and Young Persons Service, nominated several other factors that led to the radical change towards a restorative philosophy.

- There was a growing dissatisfaction among practitioners (reflected in the wider community) about the effectiveness of work with young offenders. Practitioners laboured under the unreal expectation that they could control offending behaviour through treatment programmes. Gradually a loss of confidence in the goal of rehabilitation built up. The loss of confidence, when not explicit or recognised, was often expressed as failure to resource the work adequately, a marked lack of enthusiasm for doing the work at all, and advocacy for ill-defined preventative work directed towards at-risk young people with all its net-widening effects.

- There were new and more determined efforts by Maoridom to secure self-determination in a monocultural legal system that demonstrably discriminates against Maori and places little value on Maori customs, values and beliefs. The Maori renaissance contributed, in turn, to a renewed awareness of the plight of Pacific Island cultures in New Zealand society.

- Related to Maori concerns, but also an issue for the wider community, was the growing rejection of the paternalism of the state and its professionals, and a need to redress the imbalance of power between the state and its agents and individuals and families engaged by the criminal justice system.

- Sixty years of paternalistic welfare legislation had little impact on levels of offending behaviour. Costly therapeutic programmes that congregated young offenders, particularly in residential settings, emerged as part of the problem rather than as part of the solution. Decarceration and de-institutionalisation became the buzz words for both those seeking to free up locked-in resources for other uses and those seeking more positive outcomes for individuals.

- Concerns emerged for more decided justice, in both process and disposals. Courts were beginning to dismiss cases where prosecuting authorities had failed to exercise strict procedural safeguards in the questioning and/or arrest of juveniles; the indeterminate guardianship order as a response to the serious young offender was being used less and less. Increasing numbers of young offenders were being sent to the adult court for sentence (over 2000 in 1988), an indication of the inability of the juvenile system to deal with them effectively.[9]

Doolan also points out that previous diversions schemes for young offenders often had the opposite effect of what was intended: they ended up in more trouble rather than less. They had been largely constructed around panels of officials and professionals – the Children's Boards and Youth Aid Conferences – and functioned as quasi-judicial bodies. They have always been by-passed whenever police exercised their powers of arrest. With more than 60 percent of young offenders appearing on arrest, less than 40 percent of those who appeared had been considered for a diversion option. Worse still, there was evidence that the diversion mechanisms were having a net-widening effect, by drawing into their ambit very petty offenders who should and could have been handled in much less formal ways.[10]

The new Labour government of 1984 determined to overhaul what was clearly a leaking and creaking system. They appointed a working party that year to investigate how best to change the policy and process of dealing with young offenders. The party issued a working document in December 1984, which resulted in new legislation being introduced in December 1986. This proposed legislation met with widespread criticism, especially from Maori and Pacific Island leadership. It was also criticised by professionals for being top-heavy and bureaucratic.

The government listened and, when re-elected in 1987, set up another working party to advise a parliamentary select committee on how the bill needed to be changed. This committee travelled all over Aotearoa, listening to submissions on marae and from Pacific Island groups as well as from the general public.

The result was that at the second reading in Parliament in 1989 the bill reflected a whole new approach to juvenile offending, which later that year was passed into the Children, Young Persons and Their Families Act. This act is a tribute to the possibilities Parliament has to offer this country when time is taken for consultation and proper due process.

Success Rate

The beauty of the restorative justice policy and process introduced by the act is that it works in the vast majority of cases. Not only does it place responsibility clearly with offenders to deal with their own behaviour and its effects, but it encourages and empowers families to work together to overcome difficulties. In as much as at-risk families need some legislative framework within which to operate, this act provides it. A 90 percent agreement rate at family group conferences is testimony to the ability of parties to resolve most cases of youth offending. The mechanism used is a negotiated settlement rather than an imposed solution from the top.

It should be noted that not all juvenile offending ends up immediately with a family group conference. Some serious offenders are arrested by police in much the same way that adults are. They are then brought to the Youth Court. Then, if the charge is admitted, an FGC is held within 14 days. If it is admitted and the youth is remanded in custody, it is held within seven days. If the youth has initially pleaded not guilty but the charge has been proven in a Youth Court, an FCG is then held.

Maxwell and Morris researched the effects of the act in its first three years of operation and their findings were very positive. They found that 95 percent of young people are being made accountable for their anti-social and criminal actions. This is a remarkable figure. Sanctions evolving from the FGCs include apologies and active penalties such as fines, reparation, donations to charity, community work, work for the victim, driving disqualification and curfews.

Court appearances have plummeted. From a rate of something like 64 per 1000 young people appearing in court each year, it has dropped to 16. A third of young offenders used to appear in the court. Now it is only 10 percent, and the proportion who receive court orders has also decreased. Of the 10 percent who appear in court, only 5 percent actually end up with court orders because the court accepts the recommendation of the FGC. Residential custody is also far less common – less than half the previous figures – and the length of residential sentences has been decreased enormously. Now only about 2 percent of young offenders end up with a residential sentence, which is an astonishing transformation.[11]

There are many other positive qualities associated with this restorative process. In most cases, the family group conference is convened in half the amount of time that it used to take to get an case heard in the court. It is also much more culturally sensitive, with whatever is culturally appropriate being the norm. That is a massive change inside a short space in time. The involvement of families is a crucial concept. Often families are at their wits end as to how to deal with a particularly anti-social member. The group conference can often strengthen their resolve and determination to persevere.

The family involvement will obviously have appeal to those conservative political and church groupings in the community who are strong in promoting traditional values. Often for such groups punishment has been seen to be the primary way of coping. Now there is a new mechanism that strengthens the whole bonding network of the family.

Official post-election papers from the Justice Department in December 1993 indicated that the number of prosecuted cases for defendants aged 17, 18 and 19 years had dropped by 27 percent in the five years from 1987-92. Clearly the youth justice process, while not solely responsible for such a marked decline in offending, played a significant if not a dominant part.[12]

It has to be noted that not all family group conferences succeed. In a small number of cases the whole process become a complete fiasco. Victims remain in a 'hanging' mood and veto all attempts at reasonable sanction. Offenders sometimes remain arrogant and unmoved. Families sometimes fight and squabble among themselves and are unable to reach consensus. Bearing in mind that many families are almost dysfunctional, that some have a history of neglect, drugs and violence going back years, and that some have very few social skills in terms of relationships, it should come as no surprise that such is the case. But the failure of the few should not detract from the success of the many.

Conclusion

Many claim that the restorative process adopted with juvenile offenders in Aotearoa is the most important positive piece of social legislation adopted in a generation. This claim is not misplaced. That the dominant Pakeha culture chose to learn from Maori and other Polynesian traditions and apply the lessons to the whole community, regardless of race, is cause for pride.

It is early days yet for the Children, Young Persons and Their Families Act. It will need protection from hard-line elements in the community who lust for blood and have done in every century. It will need fine-tuning as experience throws up new insights that will improve it.

It will be hard – if not impossible – to prove its strengths to the doubters because its strengths will be in its promotion of personal responsibility among young offenders, their maturation into young adults, the strengthening of family ties and community bonds, and its positive flow-on effect to a rising generation of children. In time it will be easier to see its impact on crime rates and imprisonment numbers. But such bald statistics will never tell the full story of its impact.

It has been a radical step and obviously a positive one. Now other countries are looking at our model of restorative justice among juveniles with an eye to reviewing their own systems. It leaves open the possibility that if such a philosophy works so well for adolescents, could it not also work for adult offenders?

Footnotes

1. John Braithwaite, 'What Is to Be Done About Criminal Justice?', *The Youth Court In New Zealand: A New Model of Justice*, Legal Research Foundation, Publication No 34, 1993, p37

2. F. W. M. McElrea, panel discussion, *The Children, Young Persons and Their Families Act – A Blueprint to Be Applied to Adults?* New Zealand Law Conference, Wellington, 1993, p2

3. Deborah Hollings, ibid, p9

4. Deborah Hollings, ibid, p10

5. Gabrielle M. Maxwell and Allison Morris, *Family, Victims and Culture: Youth Justice in New Zealand*, Social Policy Agency and Institute of Criminology, Victoria University, Wellington, 1993, p92

6. Ibid, p88

7. Braithwaite, op cit, p39

8. Ibid, pp37-38

9. M.P. Doolan, 'Youth Justice – Legislation and Practice', *The Youth Court in New Zealand : A New Model of Justice*, Legal Research Foundation, Publication No 34, 1993, pp19-20

10. Ibid, pp21-22

11. Gabrielle M. Maxwell, panel discussion, *The Children, Young Persons and Their Families Act – A Blueprint to be Applied to Adults?* New Zealand Law Conference, Wellington, 1993, pp5-6

12. Justice Department papers to Minister of Justice, December 1993

CHAPTER EIGHT

Aboriginal Australia: Betwixt and Between

An Aboriginal man charged with murdering his de facto wife wanted legal history made in his bid to get the Supreme Court of Western Australia to recognise the bona fides of tribal law. Neville Gable, 36, has asked the court to release him from custody so that other members of the Wongi people can fulfil tribal law and punish him by spearing him in the upper legs. Gable, a camp-dweller at Nannygoat Hill in Kalgoorlie, is charged with murdering his de facto wife by stabbing her in the throat with a knife at Ningomia Village, an Aboriginal settlement near Kalgoorlie, on 12 June 1993.

Last Monday, Gable asked Judge Yeates to release him on bail so he could be subject to the traditional spearing. Once completed under police supervision, he would return to custody to await the preliminary hearing of the murder charge against him. A Wongi elder, Mr William Wesley, told the court on Monday that if Gable was subject to the punishment, a senior male member of Gable's family would supervise the spearing to ensure that it did not get out of hand. Otherwise, brothers of Gable would be punished but without supervision. The court rejected his application for temporary bail.

The Australian, *3 September 1993*

It ill behoves a non-Aboriginal to try to give an overview of Aboriginal customary laws. For a non-Australian, an occasionally visiting New Zealander at that, to attempt this complex task appears cheeky at best and somewhat arrogant at worst. Given the fact that there are more than 700 languages and tribal groupings spread over almost the entire continent of Australia, such a challenge would seem to be too much for even a taskforce of the most eminent scholars.

This is therefore merely a modest attempt to indicate some of the outline of traditional, restorative Aboriginal law and justice. I am not trying to teach anything at all to the more than 265,000 Aborigines who belong to these tribes. Studied properly, their 40,000-year history can teach Westerners much that our own cultures have lost.

It is interesting to note that the Constitution of Australia does not mention Aborigines, nor does it protect their rights as the indigenous people of the continent. Neither does the legal system within Australia guarantee Aborigines the right of self-determination within the nation.[1]

It should also be noted that there are two indigenous peoples in Australia, the Aborigines and the Torres Strait Islanders. It is principally upon traditional Aboriginal customary law and practice that this chapter will focus.

Offending Within the Tribe or Clan

Despite some apparent illustrations to the contrary, formal gatherings in the nature of law courts did not happen in early Aboriginal Australia. They have no system parallel to that which white Australia adopted upon colonialisation, and as generally understood in modern city states. But their councils did have authority to discipline erring members and they appear to have functioned with some similar philosophy aimed at restoring the wellbeing of the community.

Such councils of elders seem to have been fairly common, but generally they are exceedingly informal and while they meet to settle disputes, among other things, they do not try to handle all types of these, nor do they always act in a judicial capacity.[2]

In researching this chapter I found that it is primarily to anthropologists that one must go for information pertaining to traditional customs and law. Probably the most accomplished team of anthropologists Australia has produced in the area of Aboriginal traditions are Ronald and Catherine Berndt and it is from their writing, spread over nearly five decades, that much of the material is drawn.

The Berndts' research indicates there are generally two categories of offending within the tribe or clan. Breaches of sacred law, that is, regulations, taboos, codes of behaviour that are thought to have a clearly supernatural basis form one clear grouping. The second comprises offences against people or property.

Given the variation in tradition that exists among the 700 tribal groups, it is difficult to pinpoint consistently applied processes whereby disputes are resolved. Ronald Berndt speaks of the seemingly casual meetings that frequently occur on the men's sacred ground, a little distant from the main camp. He has been present at many of these gatherings, at which discussion ranges from the trivial to sacred secret matters, including resolution of dispute.

The most serious disputes are said to be instigated by 'women and corpses'. The first points to a wide range of 'causes', including jealousy, adultery, elopement and so forth. The second relates to the search for a scapegoat upon whom blame may be laid for a death, with subsequent retaliation or punishment. Some of the procedures whereby a decision is made (such as inquest or divination) or retaliation takes place (for instance a revenge expedition or sorcery) are institutionalised means of resolving difficulties at the social rather than at the purely personal level.[3]

He gives a good illustration of a more formal council hearing, a type of 'court', which he heard of while doing research in 1942-43 in the lower River Murray area in South Australia among the Jaraldi.

The general term for council was *janarumi*, meaning discussion or talk. All positions were elective. Not only middle-aged and elderly but also younger men were eligible; and all adults, women as well as men, were entitled to participate. In some cases women took a leading part, but they were not usually elected to the council.

Inter-clan matters were dealt with by the relevant council: these were mainly minor disputes relating to the collection of food, fishing expeditions and so forth. Occasionally the large 'tribal' council would meet, to resolve such matters as inquest (who was responsible for someone's death), elopement, occasional instances of theft, sorcery accusations, sending out trading parties or receiving strangers from other tribes, settlement of inter-clan arguments or fights, choosing men to attack other tribes (only on rare occasions, and usually as revenge expeditions), deciding where and when a series of ceremonies was to be held and which members of adjacent tribes were to be invited, or planning an initiation ritual.

The headman would open the session by asking those present why they had come together, urging them to speak out and not to hide things so that the matter could be settled. Older men, it is said, always spoke first: they 'started up the meeting so that the younger ones might keep it going'.

The following is a construct accounts in loose translation from the Jaraldi:

> When the leader hears people talking about one man who is said to have bruised another (by sorcery), he gathers together the people concerned for questioning. When all have come, they begin to talk. An intermediary takes the part of the man who is brought before the court. There is a discussion among those for and against the accused. The women try to sift the actual facts of the case. The leader and chief adviser listen. Then he tells the people, 'Quiet, stop talking. I am going to go over this matter so it may be settled.' He speaks while they listen. Then the meeting continues.
>
> Some people support the accused: the plaintiff and his friends protest, insisting 'that one is the murderer'. The accused may deny this, avowing he murdered no-one, that he made no *naduni*, that he speared no-one with *nildjari* (a pointing bone). When all have spoken the chief headman calls out 'that is good'. He then passes judgment, finding the accused guilty or not guilty.[4]

Berndt reports that often the penalty for such offences was a thrashing or banishment from his own clan – the guilty party might be compelled perhaps to live with his mother's relatives, where he would have few rights. A high proportion of cases brought before the courts concerned sorcery, mostly as a result of inquest, and those arising from elopement, adultery and promiscuity. He noted that in all these cases women played a significant part in the court process.

Two early researchers, Spencer and Gillen, wrote in 1904 of the fire ritual – *Nathagura* – among the Waramuna people of the northern tribes of Central Australia whereby old feuds were brought to an end.

> If, for example, there be two men who have had a serious dispute that has not been finally settled up, they must now meet and, so to speak, fight it out with fiery wands, after which it may never be referred to again.[5]

They go on to describe how the men rush at their opponents with flaming torches, who ward them off with clubs and spear-throwers. This ritualised settling of the dispute ensures no serious harm is done to the participants and results in the objective: the restoration of balance and peace to the tribe.

W.L. Warner writes of the ritual sequence for feud settling among the Wawalag people in the northern Arnhem Land:

> The group gathers and a hush descends on the crowd in recognition of trouble brewing. Suddenly the men who have reason to quarrel begin to exchange words. Others gather around, spears in hand. Finally leaders intervene, often using diversion and jest as a means of bringing a peaceful settlement. If one of the quarrelling men turns on the clown, the latter points a spear at him and pretends to spear him. The general loud laughter from everyone keeps the angry one from committing any overt act; and since the clown and his audience express no hostility, the offended man cannot cause trouble.[6]

Minor disputes can be settled by other forms. The Berndts explain that a first way is typified by the northeastern and western Arnhem Land *magarada* or *manejag*. There is a judicial quality in this, insofar as the major aim is the settlement of a dispute, and all interested parties are represented. But before the meeting the accused has already been judged guilty and may have even admitted culpability. Acceptance of responsibility or a guilty plea is an important feature of all restorative systems.

Although the *magarada* is spoken of as a peacemaking ceremony it is better styled 'trial by ordeal' or 'settlement by combat'. It is clear that this procedure of conventionalised retaliation is a legal one, and closely related to a system of law. As Warner mentions, a *magarada* is not held straight after an offence, but after people have had time to cool down.

The two opposing groups, painted in white clay, stand just out of spear-throwing reach. Members of the aggrieved party advance towards the opposite side in a totemic dance, then walk back again. The others do the same. Now they are ready for the 'duel'. Men of the accused group run irregularly across the ground, and with them run two men who are closely related to both sides. Spears are flung at them – but usually with the stone or iron blades removed. They can dodge, but they must not throw back the spears, or the abuse that accompanies them. This takes the edge off the injured clan's anger.

After a brief lull, the accused man or men run across the ground. This time the blades are left in the spears and flung at him one after another. Elders from both sides try to restrain the participants, warning them to keep their tempers in check. Finally the accused man's party dance across to their opponents. If they spear him in the thigh the matter is at an end and both groups join in dancing. Ideally the thigh wound is enough, but sometimes the accused is killed.[7]

The Berndts' research shows that this process has its counterparts in other regions, with a slightly different emphasis in each case. These practices include the conventional thigh wounding of the Western Desert, and among the Maryborough (Queensland) people. This type of settlement lacks the formality of legal proceedings. It lacks the embodiment of official justice with the power to regulate in the traditional Western legal sense. But the key to the proceedings is that both parties are interested in bringing about a reconciliation between the parties. It is essentially a restorative process, not a retributive one.

In all cases we have outlined, while there is so much verbal emphasis on revenge, it is plausible to infer that underlying this is a general aim of achieving order and balance. An injury is done, the status quo is upset, retaliation provides a means by which this may be restored. Peace should follow the application of law.

Offences against property are rare among Aborigines. Ownership of land is communal, and Aborigines' non-materialistic culture mean that few offend. Offences against the person are more common and are dealt with in a variety of ways. These can range from ridicule and criticism to a spearing in the thigh with a wooden spear. This is a very traditional Aboriginal mode of punishment for serious offending. Death can be the penalty for some murders.

Customary Law

What are Aboriginal customary laws, and, given the complex tribal structure, can they be systematically codified? Law professor James Crawford of Sydney and formerly Commissioner in Charge of the Law Reform Commission's Reference on the Recognition of Aboriginal Customary Laws, writes that Aboriginal customs and laws are part of an oral culture. In terms of that culture it is usual to speak of 'The Law' rather than of laws. The emphasis is on unity and immutability rather than on plurality and change. There are no written codes or statements of customary laws such as are found in some other countries.

There is a considerable amount of general anthropological discussion on Aboriginal traditions and practices, including especially marriage, kinship, hunting and fishing practices, relations to land and dispute resolution. There is no agreement by anthropologists on important issues such as, for example, whether in Aboriginal traditional communities there were institutional authority structures for dispute resolution. However, there is agreement among anthropologists that Aborigines had and continue to have a definable body of rules, practices and traditions accepted by the community.[8]

Elsie Roughsey of the Lardil tribe relates her memories of the interconnectedness of her traditions.

> Out bush there was no-one to worry you, only the laws and customs you proudly hear, see and learn to do the right thing. If you do the wrong thing, you punish yourself by *mulgree*. You forget what you are told when eating anything strange that the salt water disagrees with, you forget to wash before moving into some places you should not go with the certain smell of food ... well, you get sick or die. These laws were proved, and were passed down to the tribes.
>
> The tribal culture has been looked carefully through ... where danger lies and the wrong is done, and where protection must be guided to all who move around these areas. If you are careless and disobey the laws, there is always a trouble in the end ... the law of creation, *mulgree*, I have seen things happen, I know they were true. I have seen many sacred dangerous spots. I have seen proved of how it was done, and how a witchdoctor cures a person from being ill, and death ... also healing touch, the chanting, the brushing of special leaves by warming on the fire and carefully pressed on the sick person, and very strangely to see, the person is well all of a sudden. Many people may not believe the fact, but it is very real and it is true.[9]

The Berndts speak of Aboriginal law and customs flowing, like that of all indigenous peoples, from their understanding of the world and the interconnectedness of all of creation. The law is there to keep things in the proper balance. The Aboriginal Australian view of the world, of people and nature, was, broadly speaking, a religious one where the traditional past lived in the present, perpetuated in and through ritual and myth.

> Life was organised fundamentally in religious terms; and the deeds and pronouncements of the creative and spirit beings of the mythical past served as a 'charter' for contemporary behaviour – not merely on the ritual ground, but in everyday life.[10]

This flows on into dispute management. The Berndts explain that quarrels and fights do occur, but within set rules of killing or making peace. In traditional Aboriginal Australia behaviour is always framed in terms of the past. To put it a little differently, the mythical characters instituted a way of life that they introduced to human beings, and because they themselves are viewed as eternal, so are the patterns they set.

They point out that the dramatising of sacred mythology affirms the social identity and solidarity of those taking part. As well, the combination of positive pressures predisposes participants to accept traditional dictates of right and wrong. The sanction of religion supplies a moral basis to society's actions.[11]

The Berndts go on to explain how this translates into everyday behaviour patterns. They point out that whether they represent good or evil, mythical figures are said to have laid down precepts that people are expected to follow today. They defined the broad roles to be played by both men and women in such matters as sacred ritual, economic affairs, marriage, childbearing, death. They warned that if people behaved in such and such a way, certain consequences would surely follow: that various taboos and avoidances had to be observed and that various relatives should not be intimate with one another. They set patterns of behaviour for members of the particular social and cultural group in which their power is acknowledged.

References to this particular dimension, not limited by time, and often translated by the words 'Eternal Dreaming', underly the Aborigines' traditional reliance on a body of knowledge and belief that is relevant not only to the past, but also to the present and the future. Within this scheme is provision for change and individual interpretation. The mythical beings are believed to have been responsible not only for creating the natural species (including humans), but also establishing an Aboriginal way of life, its social institutions, its pattern of activity, and a moral order.[12]

Ronald Berndt points out that the two most distinctive elements of Aboriginal life are the maintenance of the status quo and the fact that Aboriginal society is kin-based, and so, consequently, is its law. He says that in any given conflict a person can ideally depend on a number of others to defend or assist him. The kinship system, with its set of conventional behavioural patterns, provides a frame of reference for this. It constitutes a blueprint for social action, a guide to which people are expected to conform.[13]

Kopara

An understanding of Aboriginal law requires some knowledge of how settlement was obtained for outstanding debts and duties unfulfilled. The process is called *kopara*, which means a debt must be settled in a definite standardised way. As Ronald Berndt explains:

> Because social relationships are reciprocal and not one-sided, and because of the inter-meshing of obligations, there are pressures against leaving grievances, especially major grievances, outstanding for a definite period – unless the persons

concerned are out of touch with one another. Moreover, settlement need not take the form of physical violence or the handing over of material goods. Nor is it framed simply in terms of person-to-person satisfaction, affecting only those immediately involved. The group as such displays an interest in maintaining the peace; and although this is not always achieved, mechanisms of institutionalised or, in effect, legal procedure are available – such as the *kopara*, and penis-holding.[14]

Kopara applied to debt owed after gifts had been given for a marriage, when the man's family must respond to the 'gift' of a bride; after a birth, after circumcision, and especially after a death. On these occasions, ritualised responses need to be made to maintain the accepted spiritual balance of the family and tribe. Often the debt-settling process involved sexual activity among the various parties. Anthropologist A. P. Elkin describes one such settlement.

> [When the *kopara* party arrives to seek redress for the debt, the two groups] sit around separate fires a few yards apart and discuss the old and the new *kopara*. ... A temporary exchange of wives between picked men and women takes place ... the obligations will be finally settled by each side giving a wife to a man of the other *moiety*. [15]

Another compensatory process of restoration involves the rite of penis-holding. This symbolic action involving visiting males has an acceptance and healing dimension to it; a recognition of goodwill on the part of of the participants and the forgiveness of previous grievances. Refusal to touch the penis can be construed as provocative. An appropriate relative can often stand in as a replacement for any of this sexual behaviour. For example, among the Wailbri tribe of Central Australia:

> A man publicly accused ... may try to place his penis in the hand of an actual or classificatory brother. If the latter permits this, he undertakes to plead for the accused and, should the plea fail, to fight beside him. The brother, however, cannot be forced to accept such a responsibility.[16]

Should the evidence not be accepted the matter is finished. In some ritual sequences involving grievances, a seated man may refuse to hold the penis of a visitor, thus provoking an urgent inquiry. In such instances a kinsman can offer his penis, the visitor reciprocates, and the grievance is settled. Should the accused be a woman, a different type of sexual ritual can be involved. If she is found to be *kopara*, she will offer herself to coitus to each of those who hold a grievance. Should the woman wish to evade this kind of 'payment' she too may arrange for another woman to stand in for her. The whole emphasis in this type of penalty payment is not to punish the debtor but to recognise that law has been broken and ritual is needed to restore the proper balance within the tribe.

Law Reform Commission Report

In 1986 the Australian Law Reform Commission issued its report on Aboriginal customary law. The commission rejected codification and the general incorporation of Aboriginal customary law into the general legal system of Australia, partly in response to the plea from Aborigines that their people would lose control over their laws and there would be unwarranted intrusion into or disclosure of secret matters. However, both parties did agree that in specific instances customary laws could be incorporated into general law. These would cover such areas as recognition of traditional marriage, hunting and fishing rights, distribution of property, and some parts of traditional justice and areas pertaining to criminal behaviour.

Professor James Crawford says the courts have on occasion taken customary laws of the defendant's community into account in determining whether a defence of provocation or duress was established sufficient to reduce charges of murder to manslaughter. To ensure that the law as represented by these decisions is applied fairly and consistently, the report recommended legislation expressly allowing that evidence of Aboriginal customary laws be admissible. The commission concluded that evidence of Aboriginal customary laws could be taken into account sufficiently in the general criminal law through the exercise of sentencing and other procedural discretions, and that a customary law defence was neither necessary nor desirable.[17]

However, the commission did recommend the creation of a partial defence, similar to a defence of diminished responsibility, which would operate to reduce the level of liability in particular cases from murder to manslaughter. This defence was thought to have several advantages: it would not involve condoning or endorsing payback killings or woundings, nor would it deprive victims of legal protection or the right of redress. But it would nonetheless represent a direct acknowledgment of conflicts that can occur between the general legal system and Aboriginal customary laws. It would allow the jury a role in mitigating degree of culpability, and would operate as an adjunct to the sentencing discretion.

This can best be seen in a test case decision in February 1994 in the Northern Territory. Wilson Jagamara Walker of the Walpiri tribe at Yuendumu in the central Australian desert was convicted of manslaughter for stabbing to death a fellow tribesman. The Chief Justice of the Northern Territory, Brian Martin, gave the victim's family six months to suffer a traditional punishment instead of going to prison. In this case the man was to be speared in both thighs. At the completion of six months, if the traditional 'payback' punishment had occurred, the court would have considered justice to have been achieved.

The Law Reform Commission also reviewed the desirability of developing mechanisms within Aboriginal communities to deal with criminal justice matters.

It concluded that this time no such recommendation should be made, but did set out some broad guidelines should it be deemed appropriate to develop such a parallel system of justice in the future. These included:

• The Aboriginal group concerned should have the power to draw up local bylaws, including bylaws incorporating or taking into account Aboriginal customs, rules and traditions.

• Appropriate safeguards need to be establish to ensure that individual rights are protected, for example, by way of appeal.

• Bylaws should apply to all people within the bounds of the community.

• If the court is to be run by local people they should have power within broad limits to determine their own procedure, in accordance with what is seen to be procedurally fair by the community at large. In any event, the community should have some voice in selecting the people who will constitute the court, and appropriate training should be available to those selected.

• In minor matters there need be no automatic right to legal counsel, though the defendant should in such cases have the right to have someone (a friend) speak on his or her behalf.

• The court's powers should include powers of mediation and conciliation, as well as powers to order compensation to be made. A court that is receptive to the traditions, needs and views of the local people may be able to resolve some disputes before they escalate, perhaps avoiding more serious charges.

• There should be regular reviews of any such court, undertaken in conjunction with the local community.

Black Deaths in Custody

A chapter on Aboriginal Australians would not be complete without reference to the appalling number of deaths of Aborigines in custody. The final report of the Royal Commission into Aboriginal Deaths in Custody was published in 1991. The commission had investigated the deaths of 99 Aborigines in custody during the period 1980-89. Custody here includes police lock-ups, prisons and juvenile detention centres.

The report concluded that there is something dreadfully wrong with modern criminal justice in Australia when so many die in state custody. The commission noted that Aboriginal people are incarcerated in police custody at 29 times the rate of the general population, and in prison custody at 17 times the rate of non-Aborigines.[18]

The commission found that the underlying issues of Aboriginal disadvantage generally – racism, poverty, alienation, powerlessness, hopelessness, alcoholism –

contributed more significantly to the imprisonment of Aboriginal people than any degree of criminality on their part. In other words, Aborigines were in prison largely because of social and health factors.

In 1992 Amnesty International sent an investigative team to Australia to examine Aboriginal incarceration. It reported, among other important things, that:

> The criminal justice system makes Aboriginal people in Australia a group that is particularly vulnerable to the violation of their right 'to be treated with humanity and with respect for the inherent dignity of the human person', as set out in Article 10 of the International Covenant on Civil and Political Rights.[19]

They found that Aborigines were discriminated against according to some UN conventions. This is structured racism, and was consistent with the 1991 Report into Racist Violence conducted in Australia by the Human Rights and Equal Opportunity Commission. Amnesty International remains concerned that Aborigines continue to be subject to extremely disproportionate levels of incarceration and criminalisation. The title of its report, 'A Criminal Justice System Weighted Against Aboriginal People', aptly summarised its conclusions.

Reflecting on these stark findings, New South Wales judge Pat O'Shane comments that the picture today is as bleak for Aborigines within the dominant justice system of Australia as it was 15 years ago, and is not improving. She points out that Aboriginal Australians are over-represented in the criminal justice system, not only in comparison with non-Aborigines, but also in comparison with the world's other indigenous populations. She quotes Paul Wilson's research that shows where alienation from land occurs, extreme poverty, despair and violence develop. These have become endemic in Aboriginal communities.

Referring to racism in Australia, she points out that the objective evidence is that Aborigines suffer harsher penalties in courts than non-Aborigines from judicial officers, judges and magistrates.[20]

Conclusion

Reviewing the evidence on Aboriginal justice in Australia, one is left with the feeling that within their own communities a balanced approach to the preservation of family and tribal mores is maintained to a high degree. Traditional Aboriginal law has evolved over the more than 40,000 years that their people have lived in Australia.

As with all indigenous peoples, the protection of the tribe and the strengthening of family ties are paramount in their social rules and regulations. Their general approach to justice issues seeks to heal and restore breaches of community laws and values, even if at times their methods of doing so appear to the outsider to be somewhat harsh.

However, none of it is as harsh as what they undergo when they come into contact with the mainstream dominant culture and its justice system. The advent of the colonial system of government and its accompanying retributive system of criminal justice has brought devastation to Aboriginal communities. Aborigines are severely oppressed, as is confirmed by the findings of the Amnesty International report.

Footnotes

1. *Reconciling Our Differences*, ed Frank Brennan SJ, Aurora Books/David Lovell Publishing, Melbourne, 1992, p2
2. W.L. Warner, *1937-58, A Black Civilisation*, Harper, New York
3. Ronald and Catherine Berndt, *Aboriginal Man in Australia*, Angus and Robertson, Sydney, 1975, p176
4. Ibid, pp177-80
5. Spencer and Gillen, *The Northern Tribes of Central Australia*, Macmillan, London, 1904
6. W. L. Warner, op cit
7. Berndt, *The World of the First Australians*, Aboriginal Studies Press, Canberra, 1992, pp350-51
8. James Crawford, 'The Recognition of Aboriginal Customary Laws: an Overview', published in *Aboriginal Perspectives on Criminal Justice*, Institute of Criminology, Sydney, 1992, p84
9. Labumore: Elsie Roughsey, *An Aboriginal Mother Tells of the Old and the New*, McPhee Gribble Penguin Books, Victoria, 1984, p179
10. Berndt, *Aboriginal Man*, op cit, p174
11. Berndt, *The World of the First Australians*, op cit, p336
12. Ronald Berndt, *Australian Aboriginal Anthropology*, University of Western Australia, Perth, 1970, pp216-7
13. Berndt, *Aboriginal Man*, op cit, p169
14. Ibid, p190
15. A.P. Elkin, 'The Kopara, the Settlement of Grievances', *Oceania*, Vol II, No 2
16. M.J. Meggett, *Desert People*, Angus and Robertson, Sydney, 1962
17. James Crawford, op cit, pp65-66
18. *Final Report of the Royal Commission into Aboriginal Deaths in Custody*, 1991
19. Amnesty International, Australia, *A Criminal Justice System Weighted Against Aboriginal People*, January 1993
20. Pat O'Shane, *Aboriginal Perspectives and Criminal Justice*, Instituite of Criminology, University of Sydney, 1992, pp3-6

CHAPTER NINE

Western Samoa: Both Systems

A village chieftain was shot dead in front of his wife and five children on the orders of fellow chiefs in a small village here, Police Commissioner Galuvao Tanielu said on Wednesday. After killing Nu'utai Fatiala Mafulu, residents of the village of Lona in Fagaloa District east of here burned his home, shop, bus and pickup truck.

State-run Samoa Broadcasting Service said that Nu'utai was ordered killed because he opposed a night curfew and had not paid village council dues. Formerly, Nu'utai, who came from a family headed by a *matai* known as Matautia, had taken several legal actions against the village and the district, and was banned from both for life. Eight months ago he indicated he wanted to return and sent members of his family to make peace overtures.

AFP, 27 September 1993

The death in September 1993 of former Auckland taxi driver Nu'utai Fatiala Mafulu stunned Western Samoa and the Samoan community in New Zealand. The shooting took place at Lona in the northeast of Upolu Island. Cries of outrage greeted this deliberate killing. Questions immediately were raised as to how a village council of chiefs – a *fono* – could allow things to get so out of hand as to condone the killing of one of their own. It brought the Village Fono Act, under whose powers the chiefs claim to have been acting, into centre-stage spotlight.

An MP and former Samoan Minister of Justice, Ulualofaiga Talamaivao Niko, called for the arrest of the Prime Minister on the grounds that his party had been in power when the Village Fono Act had been passed in 1990. Under the act, *fono* were given the complete authority to deal with village justice, using the centuries-old system based on custom. The act does not define crimes or punishments or limit village chiefs' authority. Clearly, everyone agreed, the *fono* had over-reacted.

Nu'utai had lived in Auckland for 20 years but he longed for a return to his native village. Eventually, after peace overtures to the village elders, he was allowed to return with his wife and five children.

He built a shop and a bus shelter in the village. Tensions arose before the killing because of his apparent lack of respect for the traditions of the village and the position of the *matai*. A senior chief of Nu'utai's *'aiga* was disciplined by the *fono* over a land dispute and thereafter treated as an outsider. This, added to the apparent flouting of customs in the village, led things to boiling point, and the death of Nu'utai Fatiala Mafulu.

Subsequently, 41 people from the village were initially charged over the murder. Eleven charges were later dropped, and 24 people pleaded guilty to arson. The 37-year-old who fired the fatal shot was convicted of murder in March 1994. His death sentence was commuted to life imprisonment, effectively 10 years with parole. In April 1994, six *matai,* aged between 52 and 77, were charged with murder. They were alleged to have been at a Lona Village *fono* that passed a resolution that Nu'utai Fatiala Mafulu be killed and his home and property burnt. However, in October 1994 the murder charges were dropped and lesser charges of inciting others to damage a dwelling were substituted.

History

Western Samoa is a country with three sets of traditions, which often leads to clashes of values and customs. Traditional Samoan culture now blends in with major influences from European and Christian traditions. The origins of the people stretch back about 3000 years and are similar in many respects to other Polynesian communities living in the Pacific. Social structures have evolved over the centuries and, until the arrival of European immigrants in the early 1800s, centred on each independent village.

A people of the land and of the sea, Samoans' subsistence diet was culled from their crops and from the water. Land has always been a cause of great dissension among Samoans, with individual families rather than tribes having title. They also had a complex set of relationships with members of other villages. There was a complex set of titles to signify the importance of their elders, male and female. Lineage has always been important in Samoan life.

Far from being an isolated community, the Samoan village was the scene of frequent comings and goings. People engaged in such activities as the exchange of mats, the selection of titleholders, the celebration of births and the performance of funeral rites. It was in the course of this village visiting that Samoans expended much of their energy and resources and found much pleasure and pastime.[1]

Often there were matters of 'law and order' to be dealt with and the *fono*, consisting of the chiefs from all the families, was the decision-making body. In the 19th century, when there was usually no effective central government of any kind, the village itself was largely responsible for keeping order.

Some of the steps taken to achieve this end could be severe. For example, when a village was irreconcilably divided on any important issue, local or otherwise, the weaker party might be driven out in order to restore village unity. Individuals who committed serious offences were treated no less harshly. When travellers or visitors stirred up trouble or acted disrespectfully towards the village, even unintentionally, they were liable to immediate attack and expulsion by the 'aumaga' (a group of untitled men).

The Samoans were so sensitive about village honour and the enforcement of local customs and regulations that their reaction against transgressors was liable to be hasty and violent. From the local point of view, these measures were about the only ones that could have been taken, and in so far as they freed the village of divisive elements, they were effective.[2]

Samoans are not a warmongering people and often went to great efforts to avoid war between villages. However, when a village's honour was at stake because of some serious affront, war became a possibility. Two principally positive non-violent methods were used to prevent this happening if at all possible.

The first was to offer compensation, together with a formal gesture of self-degradation (ifoga). To perform the ifoga, the highest chiefs of the offending village had to go to the offended village that threatened aggression and there, on the malae, bow down and offer fine mats and the humbling of their dignity in satisfaction for the offence. Since this gesture was the greatest loss of face that a Samoan could suffer voluntarily – out of all proportion to the seriousness of most transgressions – it was never viewed lightly by either party to a dispute. A village would often choose to flee, leaving its houses and plantations to be destroyed, rather than apologise so abjectly.

When an ifoga was undertaken it was customary that the other party would accept the gesture and agree to a peaceful settlement. The whole idea of the ifoga is for the offending party to say to the offended, 'here we are, you can do anything you want with us'. The firewood and stones the offending party took with them symbolised this.

The other means of preventing war required the presence of a neutral party to stand between the disputants and propose terms of peace.[3]

Ifoga is still very much at the heart of judicial process today. The word literally means 'to bow'. An offender's entire extended family will sit with mats over their heads outside the home of a victim in a display of submission. This act of humiliation will almost always lead to reconciliation, which is at the heart of the concept. The offender is forgiven by the one wronged and reconciliation occurs.

When war had been fought between the men of the villages on neutral ground, at the point where honour was deemed to have been satisfied by mutual agreement, a formal meeting of reconciliation might then be held, officially ending the conflict. Sometimes, however, a much stronger party would simply overwhelm the adversary and loot and burn the village of the defeated. Much of the fighting was aimed to preserve village autonomy and self-respect. Independence and self-management are very important traditions for Samoans.

Local Government

There are two categories of chiefs in Samoa – the *ali'i* and the *tulafale*. Leaders of families within both are called *matai*, but their ranking is quite different. Malama Meleisea writes that the *ali'i* titles form links in the historical genealogies of the Samoans that go back to Tagaloa-a lagi.

In this respect *ali'i* titles were sacred titles that carried with them the mana of the gods. The rank of *ali'i* titles was also determined by descent from the gods – the older the title and the closer its origin to the sacred ancestors, the greater its *mana* and the higher its rank.

Tulafale titles did not depend on mana or sacred ancestry, although they originated from the same ancestral origins as *ali'i* titles. They were executive titles and carried with them special duties, which varied from family to family and village to village. Some were associated with service to an *ali'i,* some with war, or house-building, or carrying messages, or leading fishermen, or hunting, or reciting historical knowledge and many, many other roles.

Ali'i and *tulafale* had different roles in the government of villages. The role of the *ali'i* was to make the final decisions after listening to the advice of the *tulafale*, who spoke for and issued orders for the *ali'i*.[4]

All *matai* had authority over their extended families, which, in groups of up to 30, constituted a traditional Samoan village. Through marriage, all Samoans belonged to several extended families. At the centre of authority in the village sat the *fono* – council of *matai* – which made all the major political, food production and judicial decisions. Here decisions were made through negotiation, debate and compromise.

The *fono* made the laws of the village and if these were broken, the *fono* would decide how law-breakers were to be punished. They could exile a wrongdoer from a village or order the *aumaga* to beat him or inflict some other punishment such as forcing him to sit in the sun for long periods or to chew the burning teve root.[5]

Today, *fono* in the villages operate under the 1990 Village Fono Act and remain responsible for maintaining order and customs. They traditionally fine villagers for breaches of protocol and customs with penalties of money, food and fine mats.

Settler Influence

The arrival of European settlers had a massive effect on the social structure of Samoa. While there was no organised large-scale immigration, as there was to Aotearoa, missionaries and others brought news of the teachings of Jesus.

Missionary societies were established to send pastors, priests and ministers to the islands to evangelise. Christianity was rapidly accepted by the people to the point where they were able upon Independence in 1962 to write into their Constitution the famous dictum *Faavae' i le Atua Samoa* – Samoa, founded on God.

Earlier Samoa came under the influence of the three great Pacific powers of the day, Britain, Germany and the United States. They snapped and snarled at each other over who would take over the islands and rule, and in the 1880s nearly went to war over the issue. Prior to this, the Samoans had asked the British to establish a protectorate over Samoa. Britain said it was only really interested in annexing Samoa, not offering it protectorate status. So the United States was asked, but it declined, being interested only in establishing a naval base at Pagopago Harbour. In 1889 the Berlin Act was passed, by which agreement the three major powers would jointly rule the Apia area through a joint council.

Germany had long held business interests in Samoa and had control of large areas of land. It brought in a considerable number of indentured labourers from Melanesia and China. By 1900 Germany took full control and officially colonised Samoa. Germany then maintained a colonial hold over central government until 1914 and the outbreak of World War I when New Zealand, at the behest of the British government, assumed control. The change in government was to make little difference to the quest by some for more centralised government and control.

The Rule of Law

Partly because land-grabbing had led to so many disputes among the people and partly because of inter-family disputes over titles, the German Administrator in 1903 instituted the Land and Titles Commission. This was the first major effort this century to centralise law. The intention was that this body would solve all remaining land and title disputes among Samoans. It consisted of four colonial officials and 14 Samoan advisers. In setting up the commission, the administrator sought to undermine the traditional Samoan decision-making process by rearranging the power positions of the *matai*. This move struck at the very heart of the order and degree of chiefly power.

The administrator reinforced his power at an important gathering of all the Samoan chiefs. He denied them permission to hold the gathering in a senior chief's village and instead demanded that it be held in Apia. This was a significant insult offered to the chiefs. He compounded this insult by then insisting that the same fine mats be given to each chief as if they were equals. This was a clear attempt at structural change to favour the colonial power.

This point has always been particularly difficult for foreign observers to appreciate, since they tended to see 'fine mats' as economic objects in themselves, as a form of money or capital. The apparent obsession of Samoan chiefs with 'fine mats' has thus often been interpreted as irrational greed. But *'ie toga* were not a form of money in the modern sense. Although *'ie toga* could be given in 'payment' for services such as house building or canoe making, there was no set 'price' for such services. The *'ie toga* was presented with the same ceremony as on any other occasion to honour the skill of the craftsman. In Samoan eyes, the number of *'ie toga* offered represented not objects but qualities – respect, prestige, gratitude, deference, recognition, obligation and so on.

A Samoan chief of paramount rank could not therefore give equal recognition to all the district chiefs. This would insult those who historical and genealogical connections to the *Mata'afa* title had caused them to render the greatest service, or whose rank entitled them to the greatest rewards. It is precisely for this reason that gifts, in Samoan etiquette, are always publicly announced. Gifts make statements about relationships and about the nature of obligations, commitments and ties between givers and receivers.[6]

Eventually, after further liberalising changes this century, the commission was to remain as a permanent tribunal to arbitrate on matters of custom. Samoans have been encouraged to go to the commission for such judgments as are needed, but the tension remains as often those judgments are in conflict with local opinion.

Traditional Justice

This attempt to centralise village power and break down local decision-making, particularly in matters relating to justice, continued right up until Independence. Village *fono* began in the early part of this century to reassess their role in the maintenance of community relations and justice within the village. They set out rules and procedural guidelines to protect village interests. For example, when a trader ignored village rules and customs, they would punish him through sanctions and boycotts.

This produced the wrath of the central administration. One instance early this century (that has echoes in the death of Nu'utai Fatiala Mafulu) concerned a trader named Stopfkuchen, who ran a store in Salelologa in Savai'i. The *fono* ordered a boycott of his store because of his flouting of village customs. As a result of his complaint to the central administration, two *matai* were imprisoned and the *fono* warned against any repetition of such rulings.[7]

It should be noted that this occurred long before Samoans regained control of their own country and even longer before the Village Fono Act was passed.

In 1917 Logan, the New Zealand military ruler, issued a proclamation reiterating the primacy of centralised law and urging the *fono* to be temperate in their dealings with local people. Samoans responded by quoting their principle that all village rules were made by the *fono* with the intention of maintaining peace and the *mamalu* (dignity) of the community.[8]

What is of significance here is the notion that what is important to and constitutes 'fairness' in European eyes, may not have the same importance for Samoans, and vice versa. Meleisea explains:

> ... the system under which Germans and New Zealanders lived (in Samoa) was supported by an ideology of the priority of individual rights. The Samoan system was equally supported by an ideology of the priority of the collective interests of the *'aiga* (extended family) and the *nu'u* (gathering of the people). The system therefore did not admit the notion of one individual wronging another. When an individual transgressed the system, the blame, punishment and shame were shared collectively by the *'aiga*. Where the transgressor was untitled, his or her *matai* took formal responsibility.
>
> Relative evaluation as to the fairness or severity of a punishment can be determined meaningful only in the context of the values and ethics of the society whose law has been broken. For Samoans, the deliberations of the *fono* were the means of achieving decisions acceptable to all the *'aiga* that comprised the *nu'u,* even for those *'aiga* being punished. Very severe punishments, such as banishment, were decided by consensus in the *fono* where no reconciliation between parties was possible.

Banishment could never have been imposed by a minority because it had to be supported by the threat of violence from the *aumaga* if the decision was not obeyed. Force involved the pulling down of the house of the family who were under banishment orders, and destruction of their crops. In many cases the family facing social and political isolation would voluntarily accept such orders without the need for force. Banishments were seldom permanent and could revoked after formal ceremonies of reconciliation.[9]

Local versus Centralised Government

There has never been a consistent code of traditional rules governing the whole of Samoa. Consequently, when Independence came in 1962 and a Constitution was written, it was somewhat difficult to incorporate within the new structures a codified law that met the demands of the more than 80 percent who still lived in the villages, and the other grouping whose interest was in a more modern centralised form of government.

Several previous attempts to codify Samoan law had failed. Port laws were introduced by a British sea captain, Charles Bethune, in 1837. These sought to protect British interests and those of the London Missionary Society. They included no work on Sunday and curfew restrictions for visiting sailors. This was further developed the next year but restricted to the Pagopago and Apia harbours.

The next attempt came in 1839 from the British Consul George Pritchard, and later an attempt was made by American Charles Wilkes. Their efforts were partly to protect 'the poor Samoans', and partly to bring some recognised codes of behaviour for visiting crews. European settlers sought a renewed code in 1860 from Samoan chiefs. From that effort flowed what became known as Vaimaunga's Code. This contained 17 simple laws relating to property and trading rights, land sales, shipping, adultery, marriage, keeping the Sabbath, assault and murder, the carrying of lethal weapons, disorderly conduct and the regulation of liquor sales.[10]

Opposition grew to the code, and it was alleged that the chiefs of Vaimaunga had overstepped the mark in authorising it. The code was accepted in some places but not in others. In any event, it proved to be far from a universal centralised code; Meleisea points out that there was little evidence that its principles were enforced or taken seriously by Samoans.[11]

Consuls from Britain and later the United States and Germany sought to bring dimensions of their law to Samoa over the next 50 years, during which time municipal administrations were established. But with Europe at war little attention was paid to codifying the law of Samoa. The three governing nations were principally concerned with promoting their own interests rather than those of the indigenous people.

The Berlin Act of 1889 had failed to appreciate life in Samoa as it was lived, and had failed to come to grips with any centralised formulation of law. It did one important thing, though, and that was to establish the Supreme Court with a single Chief Justice of Samoa, to be nominated by the agreement of the three major powers. Yet despite its name, the court had limited power and most aspects of life relating to Samoans did not come under its jurisdiction. Samoan authorities retained jurisdiction over criminal matters, except where a European was involved.

In this century its powers would be greatly expanded as a United Nations Protectorate under New Zealand's administration. But clearly, in the lead-up to Independence, there were no clear lines of demarcation between traditional law and the jurisdiction of the *fono* on the one hand, and a centralised law and court system on the other.

Since Independence in 1962, Samoa has had to constantly face the dilemma of the traditional versus the modern ways of doing things. Many very articulate and educated young people wish the old traditions of decentralised government and the empowerment of chiefs and *fono* to continue on the grounds that such a system is local, practical, immediate. Moreover, centralised power leads too often to a morass of bureaucracy, inefficiency and disempowerment. For the majority of Samoans, small and local is beautiful.

The Constitution of Western Samoa embodies traditionalist principles and practices alongside those pertaining to a modern parliamentary democracy. This dual approach is a tension shared by other Pacific countries, most notably Papua

New Guinea and to a lesser extent Fiji. The Constitution had been drafted after extensive negotiations between New Zealand and Samoan leaders. The surveys done had indicated a very high level of contentment with existing village structures. At the time of Independence, 86.7 percent of the population lived, according to *fa'a Samoa*, the traditional Samoan lifestyle.

The Constitution takes precedence over *fono* law. As Sir Gaven Donne, Chief Justice and president of the Lands and Titles Court, said in a direction to the Samoan judges in 1980:

> Undoubtedly the customs and usages of Samoa in the past acknowledged the right of village councils and indeed the court to make banishment orders, but that custom ceased on 28 October 1960 when the people of Western Samoa through their representatives in a constitutional convention adopted, enacted and gave to themselves the Constitution.
>
> For several months before adopting the Constitution, over 170 of the most important chiefs and orators of Western Samoa, including the Tama-Aiga, deliberated on a Constitution and it was as a result of their deliberations and decisions that the Constitution was adopted and enacted. These leaders, who possessed wide knowledge of all the customs and usages of Western Samoa, decided that the written Constitution would be the supreme law and that any law in the Constitution that was contrary to the accepted customs and usages of Western Samoa that existed at that time completely superseded those customs and usages and that from thenceforth only the written Constitution would be followed and honoured.
>
> It is very important indeed that all Samoans understand that this Constitution is not *Papalagi* law that was imposed on Western Samoa. The Constitution was made by the highest chiefs and orators in the land and declared by them to be the supreme law of Western Samoa.[12]

One difficulty with the two legal systems is that they are based on two totally different philosophies. The centralised concept is based on English common law, which recognises the needs of the individual as paramount. From a criminal justice perspective, it is primarily retributive in nature. The traditional law is based primarily on a restorative philosophy, being principally concerned with the wellbeing of the community and the need to protect the interests of the majority. As Meleisea notes repeatedly in his study on this topic, the most important difference is in the notion of the right of the individual: an injury inflicted by one individual upon another is not seen in *fa'a Samoa,* as it is in Western law, as a case between two individuals, but as a case between two groups.[13]

Inevitably there are clashes between the rights of individuals guaranteed under the Constitution and the traditional norms of the villages as enforced by the *fono.* The Constitution, for example, is clear about the right of any individual to belong to any religion of choice, or none. But within the context of the *nu'u* and *fono*, this

129

holds little sway. Village rules are village rules, in place to protect the good of the community. And no individual can challenge the rules (as in Western democracies) with impunity. Those who do can face severe sanctions, as Nu'utai Fatiala Mafulu found out to his cost.

The Role of *Fono* Today

Much of the reaction into the death of Nu'utai Fatiala Mafulu centred on the feeling that the *fono* had gone too far in its administration of penalties rather than that the whole *fono* concept needed to be scrapped.

The *fono* system has its strengths. There are only 382 (unarmed) police in Western Samoa for a population of 170,000 people. These include 18,000 *matai* in more than 300 autonomous villages. The *fono* retain immense influence in village life. Much of the customary land, covering 80 percent of land area of the islands, is tied up with *matai* and various rankings of chief.

An article in the *Island Business Review* explains that council rulings guide almost every aspect of village life and even today are only slowly being eroded by social changes, mobility and education. Villages often broadcast public notices over national radio. They publicise the times when a curfew for evening prayers will be enforced. There are also notices advising on bans for long hair, being drunk and disorderly, playing music too loud, using dynamite for fishing or women wearing shorts.

Fono are a crucial factor in grassroots economic development. They organise community projects such as the building of schools and churches, sanitation, and security. Other groups such as women's committees and untitled youth work with councils of chiefs to promote the general welfare of the village. This co-operation helps build a strong sense of identity based on a community with collective responsibility, not an individual. The few areas where councils hold little sway are with new settlements around the capital Apia, freehold properties, and leased or government lands.[14]

Fines are paid the same day by the family acting together rather than by the offender on his or her own. Collective responsibility is the order of the day. Apologies – *ifoga* – are also an important part of many proceedings. This involves family members covering themselves with fine mats and kneeling outside the family home of the victim until the apology is formally accepted.

The village *fono* acts as law-maker and judiciary, with no right of appeal. At the same time the system allows for apology and reconciliation so that even exiles may be welcomed back with full rights.

Some argue that the Village Fono Act of 1990 should be abolished. But it would seem that the legislation only officially acknowledged the process of that ancient jurisdiction, which has operated for hundreds and hundreds of years, and that even the presence of three empires in the 19th century could not change. The police chief supports the *fono* system of justice:

> Without the *matai* system we would run into difficulties. We rely on them as an enforcement agency as long as they do not encroach on criminal legislation that police should handle. There are advantages and disadvantages with the *matai* system, but I don't think our job would function properly without them. Where there are differences the matter is often handled within the village before it reaches police. The traditional punishment is then used as mitigation in court. *Fono* are a state of control. Their authority is to keep order within their boundaries and organise community projects to benefit the villagers.[15]

The Secretary for Justice, Tuala Donald Kerslake, agrees. He says village law is more variable than the national system where the penalties are written down. For example, the maximum for rape is seven years and murder is commuted to life in prison. Its strength is that it is a system in a small area so it is easy to police. Village penalties are speedier: the chiefs meet, penalty is made, and the matter is settled that day. In the national system there are more procedures: you are questioned, arrested, charged, appear in court and plead. If you plead not guilty there are a series of adjournments and legal fees, before your case is decided. That may take months or a year. He sees the two systems continuing to co-exist.

Kerslake says it is common in the modern system for the family of the victim to ask for charges to be withdrawn because the matter has been settled traditionally. These settlements based on *fa'a Samoa* are also used in mitigation pleas during sentencing. Sometimes the victim will plead for the offender. Part of their survival has been by holding on to what has been their customs and traditions, because that is what makes them Samoan.[16]

Conclusion

Western Samoan law epitomises the clash between two philosophical bases underpinning separate law systems. When it acts with prudence and wisdom, the restorative nature of the *fono* system has enabled Western Samoa to remain relatively free of the major crime that now blights most nations. Clearly there can be excesses in its exercise of power. Clearly, too, individuals can feel aggrieved at the lack of individual rights compared with many other Western nations. But people in Western Samoa do not go hungry or homeless and are not regarded as worthless. There is a place in the society for everyone. Could this not be because the wellbeing and health of the community are the primary focus of its law?

Footnotes

1. R.P. Gilson, *Samoa 1830-1900: the Politics of a Multi-Cultural Community*, Oxford University Press, Melbourne, 1970, p47
2. Ibid, p48
3. Ibid, p49
4. Malama Meleisea, *Lagaga: A Short History of Western Samoa*, University of the South Pacific, Suva, 1987, p27
5. Ibid, p28
6. Malama Meleisea, *Change and Adaptations in Western Samoa*, University of Canterbury, Christchurch, 1992, pp33-34
7. Malama Meleisea, *The Making of Modern Samoa*, University of the South Pacific, Apia, 1987, p244
8. Ibid, p113
9. Ibid, p115
10. Ibid, p246
11. Meleisea, *Lagaga*, op cit, p33
12. *Samoan Times*, Vol 14, No 3, 23 January 1981
13. Meleisea, op cit, *The Making of Modern Samoa,* p214
14. *Islands Business Review*, November 1993, p23
15. Ibid, p24
16. Ibid, p15

CHAPTER TEN

The Celtic Tradition: Repairing the Damage

Fivefold Are Crimes:

the crime of the hand, by wounding or stealing;

the crime of the foot, by kicking or moving to do evil deeds;

the crime of the tongue, by satire, slander or false witness;

the crime of the mouth, by eating stolen things;

the crime of the eye, by watching while an evil deed is taking place.[1]

For 1500 years, up until the time of the final Tudor conquest, the Irish had their own criminal justice system. The *Brehon* Laws were based on a philosophy of restorative justice. In the preceding centuries, when the country was still in effect ruled on a federal basis by Irish chieftains and kings, Ireland had enjoyed a developed social structure well in advance of many other countries of its size. Eventually the *Brehon* Laws were destroyed and replaced with the harsh retributive system of the coloniser.

The *Brehon* Laws take their name from the Irish word *Breitheamh*, which means a judge. A *brehon* was a local jurist who arbitrated disputes and imposed sanctions on behalf of the community. He was one of the important people in the tribe or village who, along with the chroniclers and storytellers, the bards, the musicians and the clergy, was entrusted by the people to maintain their culture and traditions for their own wellbeing, so they might be handed on to future generations.

Brehon Laws covered all criminal acts, from murder and cattle theft to dog fights and trespass. Many were strictly speaking not laws at all but codes of conduct and traditions guiding people's behaviour. They were formed from generations of wise decisions and sayings of the elders and they helped knit into cohesive units the varying elements within each clan, and between the different clans.

There were simple rules of hospitality such as, 'Whoever comes to your door, you must feed him or care for him, with no questions asked.'[2] And rules of neighbourliness such as 'Notice of a hound in heat and the mad dog must be sent to the four nearest neighbourhoods'[3] helped achieve community justice and peace in profound yet very practical ways.

No man was allowed to act as judge until he had studied the full law course and passed a rigorous public examination. The course of study for judge and law-agent, respectively, was carefully laid down. The *brehon* was an arbitrator, umpire and expounder of the law, rather than a judge in the modern sense. It appears that the facts of a case were investigated and ascertained by laymen before submission to a *brehon* for legal decision. The complainant could select any *brehon* he pleased if there was more than one in his district. Every king or chief of sufficient territory retained an official *brehon*, who was provided with free land for his maintenance and acted as registrar or assessor in the king's court.[4]

There were, it seems, at least in some places and during some later periods, two types of *brehon*, the *brithem* and the *aigre*. The former was a 'maker of judgments' or an 'arbitrator'. The latter can be equated with the modern barrister or advocate. As Fergus Kelly explains in his book *A Guide to Early Irish Law*, *Uraicecht Becc* distinguishes three grades of judges.

The lowest grade was competent to decide on matters related to craftsmen and had an honour-price of seven *sets* (valuables or treasures). Above him was the judge who was competent in both traditional law and poetry, with an honour price of 10 *sets*. The highest grade was the 'judge of three languages', who was competent in traditional law, poetry and canon law and had an honour-price of 15 *sets*. The grading of judges is not found elsewhere, and may have been peculiar to the *Nemed* school. Each *tuaithe* seems to have an official judge, the *brithem tuaithe*, who was presumably appointed by the king.[5]

Liam Breatnach suggests that there were three periods covering a continuous legal tradition from the Old Irish period (c600-900AD), through the Middle Irish period (c900-1200), to the Classical Modern Irish period (c1200-1650). The end of this tradition coincided with the demise of the Gaellic aristocracy and the social system that supported it.[6]

The *Brehon* Laws governed a society that was essentially federal, not feudal. At the time eastern Europe was almost totally feudal. Because the Irish were federal their political system had not evolved with any strong centralised form of government, nor a system of universal law. It was into such a country that, over a period of centuries, wave upon wave of English armies came until, by sheer weight of numbers, the Irish were subdued.

The centralised code of English law imposed on them after the first invasion in 1169 did not take root until the 16th century, when the English applied their military screws more tightly. If there had been in Ireland a despotic monarchy, a feudal civilisation that ground down the people and exalted the nobles, it is probable that the English would have been driven out. But the Irish national genius was in harmony with a concept of freedom and humanity, which a mammon-ridden world has never known elsewhere, and through the centuries it fought obstinately for its own concept of the proper order of things.[7]

The 1603 Treaty of Melifont marked the official end of the prevailing federal clan system, and the Disarming Act of 1695 marked the temporary end of the Irish power of military resistance. The way was then open to attempt to conquer the Irish mind as well, with the Penal Laws being used as the chief instrument for this enterprise. It should be noted that during all this period, until well into the 16th century, the *Brehon* Laws held sway in the countryside and provincial towns. It was only on the eastern seaboard and especially around Dublin (within the Pale) that English law was observed to any degree prior to this. That eventually three centuries later the English left Ireland – except for Ulster – is now a matter of history. But by that time centralised government and a centralised code of law were well implanted.

Social Structure

In order to understand the breath, width and wisdom of *Brehon* Laws, it is important to have some knowledge of the social structure of ancient Ireland. It is clear that they were in universal use until the English conquest (and indeed used in parts of Ireland for many centuries later), and pertained to every facet of Irish life.

> Six cows are the fine for breaking a tribesman's two front teeth; 12 heifers for maiming a homeless man.

> For pulling off the hairs of a virgin bishop the fine is one yearling heifer for every 20 hairs.[8]

Our main information on the economic basis of early Irish society comes from the law texts. They describe a self-sufficient mixed farming economy based on the rearing of cattle, sheep and pigs and on the growing of cereals. The economic system was sustained on the inter-relationship of lord and client: the lord advanced a fief of stock or land to his clients and in return received rent and services. Sufficient wealth was generated to sustain not only a hierarchy of lords and kings, but also various professional men, of whom the most important are poets, judges, smiths, physicians and wrights (skilled workers).[9]

It was primarily a rural society. Built-up townships were few and far between, and usually constructed around a monastery. There must have also been trading settlements on the coasts, particularly in the south and east. The wisdom-text Tecosca Cormaic includes 'ships putting into port' as one of the signs of a good king. Their cargo would have included wine, fine cloth and various other luxury items. There is also evidence of the import of British horses. Little is known about exports from Ireland at the time of the law texts.[10]

Irish society generally could be divided into six classes: the kings of various grades, the professional classes, the *flaiths*, who constituted a type of nobility, freemen possessing property, freemen possessing no property (or very little), non-free classes. Progress could be made between the ranks depending on wealth accrued and qualifications.

So Irish society was hierarchical and class-based; egalitarianism was not a feature. The laws reflected this and an offence against a person of high rank carried a greater penalty than one against a commoner. While in later times Roman law and canon law would uphold equality before the law, native Irish law did not.

The whole social structure from a legal viewpoint was built upon a person's honour-price, or *log n-enech* (literally, the 'price of his face'). This had to be paid for any major offence committed against him eg murder, satire, serious injury, refusal of hospitality, theft, violation of his protection. A person's capacity to perform most legal acts was linked to his honour-price. Someone could not make a contract for an amount greater than his honour-price, nor could he go surety beyond this amount. Likewise his oaths and evidence were only given a weight commensurate with his honour-price.[11]

There were three levels to Irish social structure: the *fine*, the *sept* and the *tuath* (*clann*). The smallest organism – political and social – next to the immediate family was the *fine* (pronounced finna). It was more than a family, but it was in the family that it took its origin. It closely corresponded to our notion of extended family or whanau since in the course of time the term came to be applied to a group of kindred families, or to a joint family group of four generations.

Originally the family had its allotted portion of land, but as children and grandchildren arrived at maturity and became heads of families themselves, or at least at an age where they could inherit and possess property and share in responsibilities, the original land became divided and subdivided among them. This aggregate of individuals, freemen born, members of the same clan, deriving their descent from the same ancestor, bound together by ties of kinship and interest and possessing a common portion of land, made up the corporate body called the *fine*. At its head stood the *flaithe-fine*. He was the paterfamilias, the representative of the *fine*. He was to sue and be sued in its name, to guard its interests and defend its rights.[12]

The kin-group or *fine* is the group most referred to in the law texts. The members are all descendants through the male line of the same great-grandfather.

A kin-group possesses considerable legal power over its members. Each kin-group had its own kin-land – *fintiu* – for which every legally competent adult male in the group had some degree of responsibility. No-one could sell his share of the kin-land against the wishes of the rest of the kin.[13]

The kin-group had social responsibilities in relation to its members. It was also liable for the fines and debts of its members, so if an offender absconded, his kin became liable. If payment was not forthcoming the plaintiff could claim cattle from a kinsman of the offender, using a special form of distraint. The head of the kin was known as the *agae fine* or *cenn fine*. He was chosen – presumably by election among the kin-members – on the basis of his superior wealth, rank and good sense. He spoke for his kin on public occasions, such as an assembly or court of law, and gave pledges on behalf of his kin to ensure the fulfilment of any responsibility that any kin-members may have towards the king, Church or poets.[14]

The next level of social structure was the *sept*, which has no English equivalent but is similar to the Maori hapu. The *sept* was an intermediate organism between the *fine* and the clan. It consisted of a number of *fines*, as the clan consisted of a number of *septs*. It was one of the divisions of the clan assigned a specific part of the territory, and over it and this district a *flaithe* was supposed to preside. No rule is stated as to the number of persons or *fines* that might be a *sept*. The right of the *sept* to undisturbed possession of its assigned portion of the territory was greater than that of the *fine*, was subject only to that of the clan, and was very rarely interfered with.[15]

At the next level existed the *tuath* or *clann* (clan). Each clan was a distinct group and tried to be self-sufficient and self-contained. A clan had the land as its property. After the clan in degree of importance came the *sept*, where one existed, and then the *fine*. The individual was left little to do but fill the position assigned to him or her and conform to the system.[16]

The clan built small monasteries and schools, endowing them with lands, stock and other necessities. As a rule it dedicated every first-born son to the Church and it retained to itself the right of succession to all posts, clerical and lay, so long as it possessed qualified people. The clan had its bishop or abbot with episcopal faculties and territorial jurisdiction.

Tuath, *Cinel* and *Clann* were synonyms meaning a small tribe or nation descended from a common ancestor. A king and clan being able, subject to certain limitations, to adopt new members or families, or amalgamate with another clan, the theory of common origin was not rigidly adhered to. Kinship with the clan was an essential qualification for holding any office or property. The rules of kinship largely determined status with its correlative rights and obligations, supplied the place of contracts and of laws affecting the ownership, disposition and devolution of property, constituting the clan an organic, self-contained entity, a political, social and mutual insurance co-partnership.

The solidarity of the clan was its most important and all-pervading characteristic. According to the traditional view the entire territory occupied by a clan was the common and absolute property of that clan, a portion being set apart for the maintenance of the king. Warriors, statesmen, *brehons*, *ollamhs*, physicians, poets and even eminent workers in the more important arts were also rewarded with free lands. Rank, with the accompanying privileges, jurisdiction and responsibility, was based upon a qualification of kinship and of property held by a family for a specified number of generations, together with certain concurrent conditions, and it could be lost by loss of property, crime, cowardice or other disgraceful conduct. A portion of land called the *cumbal senorba* was devoted to the support of widows, orphans and old childless people.[17]

The law texts indicate that the basic territorial unit was the *tuath*, conveniently translated 'tribe' or 'petty kingdom'. On the evidence of genealogies and other sources, it is calculated that there were probably 150 kings in Ireland at any given date between the fifth and 12th centuries. Each of these kings would have ruled over his own *tuath* (and many others would also have been overlords of the *tuatha* of other kings). Any estimate of the total population of Ireland at this period is of course highly speculative, but a figure of something under half a million has been proposed. On this basis the average *tuath* could be reckoned to have contained about 3000 men, women and children.

According to one law text, no *tuath* can be regarded as a proper *tuath* unless it has an ecclesiastical scholar, a churchman, a poet and a king. The life of a *tuath* centred on its king: all the freemen owed him their direct loyalty and paid him a special tax. At any time the king could summon them to a *slogad* or 'hosting' to repel invaders or attack a neighbouring *tuath*. He also convened the *oenach*, a regular assembly for political, social and perhaps commercial purposes.[18]

Each clan had two local assemblies of its own for the transaction of ordinary business. One was called the *cuirmtig*, and was open to all clansmen who paid tribute (a type of tax for the wellbeing of the common good). The other was called the *dal,* and appears to have been open only to the heads of *septs*, although it may have included heads of *fines* as well. The *dal* was a type of second chamber or upper house where decisions made at the *cuirmtig* were ratified or otherwise. Each clan also had a further assembly called a *tocomra*, at which the king or chief was elected.

Of local assemblies, the *oenach* appears to have been the most important. *Oenach* is a word meaning a fair, and in effect once the assembly came together, what amounted to a cattle fair sprang up alongside. In time the *oenach* was also taken advantage of for holding a high court of justice to hear appeals, Church synods, a place for musical, poetry and bardic contests, weapon displays, athletics, horse racing and dancing. In time these supplementary activities overshadowed the original ides of a local assembly where decisions were made.

In ancient times there were two national assemblies, which brought people together from all over the country. The most important was the Feis of Tara, held every three years, which was an assembly of the leading men of the land. It was restricted to leaders – kings, *flaiths*, warriors, *brehons*, chiefs, poets, leading bards. The Feis of Tara died out in the sixth century. Another celebrated national assembly was held annually for many centuries at Tailltenn on the Blackwater in Meath. It was a general assembly of the people and was not restricted to those of rank and distinction. Its purpose was social and political, and laws were debated and enacted. This assembly lasted into the reign of King Roderick O'Connor, and was last held in 1168AD.

Up until this time the country was governed essentially by a small aristocratic ruling class, the principal titleholder being a king. Next to the kings were nobles or princes of varying grades. A wealthy person could in time aspire to become a noble if he accrued enough wealth. Theoretically even peasants could aspire to the highest office.

In practice the most important social distinctions seem to have been between those who were *nemed* (privileged) and those who were not *nemed*; and between those who were *soer* (free) and those who were *doer* (unfree). The chief categories of *nemed* in society were king, lord (*flaithe*), cleric and poet. Some texts include the physician, judge, blacksmith, coppersmith, harpist, carpenter and other craftsmen as a lower appendage of the *nemed* class. But it is clear they do not enjoy full *nemed* privileges.

Ranking below the *nemed* was the non-*nemed* freeman, who probably made up the majority of the adult male population at this period. He had an honour-price in his own right and could take independent legal action. He attended the assembly and thereby played a part, however small, in decisions affecting the *tuath*. The law texts distinguish two main categories of non-*nemed* freemen: the *ocaire* and the *boaire*, who can roughly be equated respectively with the 'small farmer' and the 'strong farmer' of 20th-century Ireland.[19]

The most important *nemed* person in a *tuath* is the king. But there could be ranking even among kings, with some acquiring dominance over other *tuatha*, receiving military assistance from them in times of war.

However, as Kelly points out, the King of Ireland who figures so prominently in the sagas, is rarely mentioned in the law texts. He says that though the idea of a kingship of all Ireland had already gained currency by the seventh century, no Irish king ever made it a reality and most law texts do not even provide for such a possibility.[20]

Under ancient Irish law the land did not belong to the king or the chief or the landlord, but to the tribe. The lowest of the free-tribesmen had as much an inalienable right to their share as had the chief himself.

One of the important things spelt out in the *Brehon* Laws was that the poor, the aged, the orphans and the widowed were to be provided for within their clan. There were detailed instructions as to how they were to be looked after. For example, law decreed that the sick were to have ample ventilation and to be provided with fresh water. Detailed regulations were spelt out governing care for the aged:

> When you become old your family must provide you with one oatcake a day, plus a container of sour milk.
>
> They must bathe you every 20th night and wash your head every Saturday.
>
> Seventeen sticks of firewood is the allotment for keeping you warm.[21]

Free clansmen, who formed a type of middle class, provided for their care. This was paid to the clan's *flaithe* or chief to oversee their wellbeing. Such tributes were often paid for in kind and one farmer would make a speciality of breeding one particular class of stock, another a different class. The *flaithe* took up the tributes from the different farmers at different seasons of the year, thus maintaining a supply for those in need. The *flaithe* was kept informed of stock levels within the *sept*. The *flaithe* was also bound to provide bulls and stallions for the use of the *sept*. These were very useful functions, and they by no means exhausted the duties which by law the *flaithe* was bound to discharge.[22]

Senchas Mar

In the 19th century two famous Irish scholars, Professors Eugene O'Curry and John O'Donovan, transcribed some ancient texts of *Brehon* Law into 17 volumes. Their study reveals not just dry and dusty ancient law texts but:

> ... thousands of details. Details that described ancient life in the days when the Irish still lived in mud huts and small ringed settlements, and paid their bills in cows and bacon, handsome gold brooches and ordinary wooden bowls: the brewer testing a grain of malt against his tooth to guard against bitterness in the ale; farmers lugging sides of beef to the chieftain to pay their quarterly rent; a pregnant wife who craves a morsel of food; mischievous boys shouting at pigs ... the Irish laws serve as a repository of primitive customs, some dating back 3000 years and most gathered by Celtic wanderers from various members of the far-flung Indo-European family.[23]

Much of the law has been lost in the mists of antiquity and much more was destroyed by the English colonists. Under the infamous Penal Laws imposed by

England, it was very risky to be caught with any Irish manuscript. Subsequent to these translations many other laws and manuscripts have been found that add to those of these two scholars.

At the beginning of the written tradition belong four important texts, the first three in Old Irish. They were the most famous of them, the *Senchas Mar*, the *Bretha Nemed Toisech*, written in Munster in the second quarter of the eighth century, and the *Cain Fuithirbe*, an earlier Munster text completed sometime between 678 and 683AD. The *Collectio Cannonum Hibernensis* was the fourth text, written in Latin in the eighth century.[24]

The *Senchas Mar* contained some of the most important traditions, customs and laws. It is regarded as the greatest work on traditional Irish law, both civil and criminal. It contains much of the law existing before the advent of St Patrick, who had a marked influence on much of *Brehon* Law. The *Senchas Mar* also included a very important section on the Law of Distress, which assumed such an important role in Irish legal history. Other volumes covered ancient laws on hostage sureties, the law of fosterage, of tenure of stock, of social connections. There were tracts on taking possession of land, tenancy, the rights to water, divisions of land, social ranks, laws relating to poets and their verse, to the Church, chiefs, pledges and other contracts.

Noted scholar D.A. Binchy suggests that another group of ancient law texts also existed. He calls them the *Nemed* (holy or privileged) collection. They contain many duties and rights of artists, poets and bards and seem to have emanated from the Munster area. There is also evidence to suggest that there were other law sources as well, and Kelly makes reference to them.[25]

Within the *Senchas Mar* there is a special treatise called the Book of Aicill. It is taken up primarily with what we now call criminal law. It comprises principally the opinions of two eminent leaders, both men of law. The first was King Cormac mac Airt (otherwise called Cormac ua Cuinn), King of All Ireland, who ruled from 227 to 266AD. He was a great reformer of national institutions in his time, including the historic Feis of Tara. A patron of literature, art and industry, he wrote (or had written) several works on law, history and other important subjects.

The second author of the Book of Aicill was Cennfaeladh, who lived in the seventh century. He was a soldier and a lawyer. He appears to have rewritten the whole work and undoubtedly modernised it, bringing it into harmony with the requirements of Christianity, which by this time had become the principle religion of Ireland. His re-editing of King Cormac mac Airt's seminal work in essence constituted a new, revised and enlarged second edition of the work.

These law traditions are all built on a philosophy of restorative justice. Reconciliation, reparation and healing, along with mercy and forgiveness, are the hallmarks of their practical application.

Irish Criminal Law

It appears that in ancient Ireland almost any crime could be dealt with by way of a fine, which seems unusual in a race known for its fighting traditions. The law texts present a fine as a possibility in practically every case, even if in many instances it was impossible for the accused to pay on his or her own. This is where the strength of the fine came into play. In spite of the absence of a state system of law enforcement in pre-Norman Ireland, it is likely that in most cases the prestige of the law and of the judge's office – combined with the system of pledges and sureties – would have ensured that the fines imposed by judges in court were actually paid.[26]

In later times there was a set procedure for the perusal of law cases. Kelly's research reveals eight stages that were followed before a decision was reached.[27] Many correspond to current law practice in modern Western jurisdictions. One could assume that such detailed procedures developed under the guidance of ecclesiastical law and were used more often for serious rather than minor cases.

There were basically three levels of advocacy. One, called a 'fettering advocate', was competent in enforcing the decisions made on behalf of the court. This one had a role that appears to be a cross between our bailiffs and police. A second role was that of 'court advocate', who pleaded a case on his own behalf. The third role was that of an 'advocate whom judgment encounters', who played a role not unlike a court lawyer today.

The practising lawyers, then, both judges and advocates, were distinguished not only according to their competence in the law, but also according to the societal and political divisions of early Christian Ireland. Judges were appointed either by church or lay authorities, and advocates acted for both laymen and ecclesiastics. Advocates were distinguished according to the status of the people they acted for, while judges were distinguished according to the political importance of the king or monastery that appointed them.[28]

On the surface there also seems to have been no hard and fast line drawn between civil and criminal offences in *Brehon* Laws. However, in practice there were some subtle but real distinctions. In civil cases the defendant often had the right to choose the judge, whereas usually in criminal cases the *brehon* was first approached, often at the instigation of the victim.

It is of profound significance to note that a restorative rather than a retributive philosophy prevailed. The laws discouraged revenge and retaliation and permitted capital punishment only as a last resort. They contained elaborate provision for dealing with crime, but the standpoint from which it was regarded and treated was essentially different from ours. The state, for all its elaborate structure, did not assume jurisdiction in relation to any crimes except political ones, such as treason or the disturbance of a large assembly.[29]

In the case of a crime committed by an individual, the *fine* and the *sept* were liable. People against whom the crimes had been committed were left to sue for redress by summoning the offender to appear before a *brehon*, who heard the case and assessed the amount of fine that should be imposed. The *brehon* had the traditional laws and standards to guide his judgment. If the defendant did not pay immediately, a levy of distress could be placed on his goods.

There were no prisons and there were hardly any public servants who could correctly be called police or detectives. The people were their own police. Their activity was sharpened by the knowledge that a *sept* had to pay for a secret crime committed in its territory, unless the crime had been committed by an outsider. This liability continued as long as the criminal lived, whether his crime was against person or property.

If the crime was purely personal the *sept* was no longer liable, for the crime died with the criminal. But if it was against property, the *sept* remained liable. Every clan and clansman had a direct interest in the suppression and prevention of crime.[30]

The strong bonding within the community, helped by a law seen to be fair and equitable towards all, meant that it was in everyone's interests to maintain and support it. The only way someone could escape the consequences of criminal behaviour was to flee. But to flee was to leave all personal property behind, which meant the *fine* or the sept would have to bear responsibility for the penalty. To escape was to become an outcast and to live as a fugitive.

Reparation was the usual method of penalty. There were several levels at which fines operated. The *brehon*'s role was to give judgment on the penalties. Fines could be paid in differing forms and combinations of them. There were varying currencies – ounces of silver, *sets* (treasures), cattle and *cumals* (literally a female slave, but more often 'a unit of value') being the most common. Cattle were most often used as payment, the basic unit being a milk cow accompanied by her calf.

> For stealing your pigs or your sheep,
>
> for stripping your herb garden,
>
> for wearing down your hatchet or wood-axe,
>
> you may take your neighbour's milk cows to the public animal pound for three days.
>
> If he does not want his cows taken to the pound for his crimes or his bad debts,
>
> he may give his son as security instead.[31]

The severest fine was the *eiric* or *eric*, a fine for murder or manslaughter. The actual amounts varied with the circumstances; for the wealthy it was far more severe than for the poor. The level of intent and malice was also a major factor. A murderer would usually pay at least twice the amount assessed for manslaughter, but it could be much more.

Honour-price as mentioned earlier was another form of fine and was determined by status. The same law that arranged the different ranks of society and fixed their respective rights and privileges and liabilities also fixed the honour-price. For criminal offences or breach of contract this honour-price was forfeited in part or in total. The whole of the honour-price would be forfeited for a murder, with reparation going partly to the injured family and partly to the king.

In the case of certain peculiarly vile crimes, the criminal was expelled from the clan and from the territory, even though the fine had been recovered. An habitual criminal might also be expelled, and by expelling him and lodging a security against his future misdeeds his relatives could free themselves from responsibility. A person so expelled became an outlaw, with no status or right whatever, no legal capacity and no protection from the law. And anyone who gave him food or shelter became liable for his crimes.[32]

Fines were accompanied by other less specific penalties. Along with the fine went the shame of offending, a sense of public humiliation, a loss of status that could include the disqualification from holding public office, from suing others, acting as a juror, inheriting land. These penalties could be short term or longer.

The principles governing the severity of an offence and penalty to be imposed were guided by four factors: the damage done, the status of the injured person, the status of the offender, the accompanying circumstances.

So, for example, a man of high rank was always fined more than a man of low rank in a like case. A property offence against a poor person would be punished more severely than if it was committed against a person of wealth. An assault against a highly ranked person was more severely punished than a similar offence against a peasant.

For large fines, the penalty could be paid in varying currency: several cows, some silver and some food could constitute the full payment. For assaults, the system ran the same way. A fine of two cows was considered heavy for a blow that did not draw blood. It was up to the *brehon* to decide.

Sanctuary

Another feature of importance contained in the *Brehon* Laws was that of sanctuary. The *maighin digona* was the area house of every clansman and within this area the owner and his family were inviolable. Rank determined the size of the sanctuary around a home. For a low-class person it was quite a small clearing; for someone of high rank it could be an area stretching up to 1000 paces. For chiefs, bishops and nobles it could be that area measured by the distance one could hear the sound of a bell, or the crow of a rooster. The owner of the *maighin digona* was empowered to extend protection to a fleeing stranger, but such sanctuary needed the owner's consent.

Murder

In the case of murder, Irish law sought compensation rather than the death sentence. This same practice of seeking reparation instead of the death penalty was also carried out by the ancient Greeks, the Gauls, the Franks, the Swedes, the Danes, the Germans and the Saxons.

It seems two main types of fine were normally paid to the victim's kin. The first was the fixed penalty for homicide, which amounted to seven *cumals* for every freeman irrespective of rank. The other main fine was based on the honour-price of the victim's kin and was distributed among both his paternal and maternal kin. If the victim was of high rank it could become a very expensive business, to which kinsmen were expected to contribute.[33]

Where the *eric* could not be paid or there were special circumstances, the family of the victim could kill an offender. But there was no state execution. There are varying opinions as to how often a retaliatory execution was carried out; it would seem to have been a relatively rare occurrence.

The *Brehon* Laws give various qualifications as guidelines for dealing with murder:

> The fine for killing a bond-person held as security for a loan (or for killing a slave) is 21 cows;
>
> for killing a free farmer of Erin the fine is 42 cows.
>
> For killing a noble the fine for homicide is paid, plus an additional amount determined by his rank in society.
>
> Fines are doubled for malice aforethought.[34]

There is ample evidence that Irish opinion was generally against the death penalty. There are several passages to the effect that no-one was put to death as long as the *eric* was obtained, and that an assailant should not be put to death if he was known or could be arrested. For high treason hanging was a possibility, and on occasion a murderer could be put into an open boat and exposed to the possibility of death at sea.

Conclusion

The philosophy of restorative justice upon which the *Brehon* Laws were based covered all criminal offending, including murder. Retaliation and retribution based on vengeance were not a part of that philosophy. The whole aim was to restore to wellbeing the victim and the community, and there is evidence of real flexibility in the way the laws were framed so as to make sure that happened.

Retribution and vengeance only came with the colonisation of Ireland by the English and the imposition of English law, which eventually saw the *Brehon* Laws disappear from the penal code of Ireland. One suspects, however, that they have not altogether disappeared from the deepest subconscious of the Irish people.

Footnotes

1. Mary Dowling Daley, *Irish Laws*, Appletree Press, Belfast, 1989, p46
2. Ibid, p29
3. Ibid, p50
4. *Encyclopaedia Britannica*, Vol 4, Encyclopaedia Britannica Ltd, London, 1959, p85
5. Fergus Kelly, *A Guide to Early Irish Law*, Dublin Institute for Advanced Studies, Dublin, 1988, 1991, p51
6. Liam Breatnach, 'Lawyers in Early Ireland', article in *Brehons, Sergeants, and Attorneys*, ed Daire Hogan and W.N. Osborough, Irish Academic Press, Dublin, 1990, p2
7. P.S. O'Hegarty, *The Indistructible Nation*, Maunsell and Co Ltd, Dublin, 1918, p48
8. Daley, op cit, p25
9. Kelly, op cit, p3
10. Ibid, p6
11. Ibid, p8
12. Monsignor D'Alton, *History of Ireland*, Vol 1, Gresham Publishing Co Ltd, London, 1925, p25
13. Kelly, op cit, p12
14. ibid, pp13-14
15. Laurence Ginnell, *The Brehon Laws*, T. Fisher Unwin, London, 1894, pp107-09
16. *Encyclopaedia Britannica*, p85
17. *The Course of Irish History*, ed T.W. Moody and F.X. Martin, Mercier Press, Cork, 1967, p45
18. Kelly, op cit, p319
19. Kelly, op cit, pp9-10
20. Ibid, p17
21 Daley, op cit, p59
22. *Encyclopaedia Britannica*, op cit, p86
23. Daley, op cit, p4
24. Liam Breatnach, op cit, p2
25. Kelly, op cit, p246
26. Ibid, p214
27. Ibid, p191
28. Liam Breatnach, op cit, p13
29. Ginnell, op cit, pp123-24
30. Ibid, pp185-86
31. Daley, op cit, p48
32. Ginnell, op cit, p191
33. Kelly, op cit, p126
34. Daley, op cit, p47

CHAPTER ELEVEN

God's Way: Biblical Justice

Scripture has a bad name when it comes to dealing with criminal justice. What person in the street, when asked what scripture has to say about crime, will not immediately think of the quote 'an eye for an eye, a tooth for a tooth'? Or quote one or other of the Ten Commandments?

That such quotes are usually taken out of context and misunderstood as a result seems to escape notice. Indeed, one might go as far as to say that the underpinning of Western law and the justification for our horrendous prison system can to a large extent be attributable to what Christians have perceived to be God's view of such matters as found in scripture.

In a study such as this, it is important to include a chapter on biblical justice because of the Christian influence on the development of a codified law in Western history and its influence on the penal system. To ignore these influences because of the secular nature of the age would be to remain blind to an influence of major significance.

In this chapter I will seek to look at the misquotes used to justify our current system, at the true nature of biblical justice, and the implications for the future if a biblical vision was enacted.

What Does Scripture Say?
The Bible appears to have much to say about crime and punishment. Naturally it deals with what flows from violations of law, and in particular with what flows from violations of its most sacred law, the Torah, which contains the commandments of God. But all law was not of equal status in biblical times. Consequently, how one dealt with offenders varied depending on a wide variety of circumstances.

There was no centralised code of law or criminal justice system such as we have now. That is something that developed in Western civilisation, and it really only started to take root in a centralised way from the 13th century. Such law is really quite a late development.

So when Jesus is accused of breaking the law on the Sabbath, rather than being arrested and charged, he merely has an argument with his accusers about the ruling itself and the nature of law, and he is left to move on.

A Jewish understanding of Hebrew law has often been quite different from a Western Christian understanding of the same law. For example, Martin Buber, the famous Jewish scholar, in his German translation of the scriptures, translates 'an eye for an eye and a tooth for a tooth' as 'an eye for the value of an eye, a tooth for the value of a tooth'.

As scripture scholar Herman Bianchi points out, there is no historical evidence that one would lose an eye as a punishment for assaulting and damaging the eye of another. The eye and the tooth notions are symbolic. (Incidentally, that particular phrase occurs only three times in the whole of scripture.[1]) The concept of *lex talionis*, the law of proportionality, simply says that you should never claim more than the value of what is damaged. If property worth 100 gold coins is stolen, then you cannot claim 200 coins in return. If you took more than what was just, then you in turn could be punished.

The emphasis was usually on restitution and restoration, not vengeance and punishment.[2] Restitution was seen as a way of setting things right. If property was stolen, then the property should be returned; if damage was done to someone's house or field, then the person responsible for the damage should repair it.[3]

Later in the New Testament, Christ specifically rejects this notion when he says quite emphatically: 'You have heard it said "an eye for an eye". But I tell you, do good to those who harm you.'[4]

The focus on crime in biblical times was not so much on individuals as on the community. Corporate responsibility was central to the Hebrew understanding of crime.

First (Old) Testament understanding renounced any scapegoating that claimed that crime was only the responsibility of a few evil individuals within the society. When the law was broken, there was corporate responsibility. Violence and breach of law pointed to a crisis in the very fabric of the society.

It is from this understanding that the prophets are able to warn that the entire nation is doomed because some widows have been mistreated or because the hungry have not been allowed to glean the fields. Not only all the people but the land itself is caught up in sin and all its consequences, for the meadows lie barren and the mountains quake and the trees bear no fruit. For Israel, the fullest response to crime was not the isolated punishment of an individual law-breaker, but the repentance of the entire nation.[5]

Herman Bianchi has pointed out that in the West we have translated the Ten Commandments as imperatives, thus losing something of their meaning in their original context. In Martin Buber's Hebrew text, the verbs express future tense, not imperatives. The Law of Moses begins with an introduction that contains a promise. Translated, it has God saying: 'I am the Lord your God. When you follow my indications, my Law, my wise ways, I will bring you freedom and life.'

> Thus the commandments are better understood as meaning: 'When you follow my wise indications, you will not steal any more, you will not kill, you will not commit adultery.' The scriptures go on to show that when the Jewish people did follow God's law they were blessed, and when they went astray, they were not. In modern terms we too can have a blessed society, when we try to break down the bureaucracies that have taken everything from us, when we give neighbourhoods another chance to live as neighbourhoods, then we won't steal any more, we won't kill any more. It is a promise. It is the promised land.[6]

The central feature of biblical law is a constant calling forth of the people to a future promise. The emphasis is on the future health and wellbeing of the community, and not on the immediate transgressions of the law. The covenant agreed to by Moses and the people with Yahweh always emphasises this future direction. It also helps explain why rabbis are constantly in debate about the meaning of the law. In some English translations it is not as clearcut and imperative in its practice as it might sometimes appear.

How then did the West come to see God as a punishing High Court judge-type figure who hovers over our everyday activities like an eye-in-the-sky policeman? This clearly is not the emphasis of the scriptures. We have done that it seems by largely misinterpreting the actual meaning of some key passages of scripture, and by failing to recognise the context within which they were written.

There are several key words in scripture that indicate the presence of justice in a much fuller sense than what we usually understand. Justice is part of the very essence of God, as can be seen from reading the psalms and the prophets, especially Isaiah, Jeremiah, Micah and Amos, and from reflecting on the Gospels. As theologian Kevin O'Reilly says:

> In the Bible God is called the just one. What is this justice of God? According to the Old Testament authors, the justice of God is not the quality whereby God rewards the good and punishes the wicked. God is just when he intervenes in the lives of the underprivileged, especially orphans and widows, to save them from the injustices of men (Deuteronomy 10/18). God is just when he defends the cause of the innocent. God is just when he establishes those who have been exploited by wicked men. God is just when he saves the poor.[7]

A key word for justice is *t'sedeka*, which Buber translates as 'to bring the truth, to be truthful, to speak the truth'. Justice, then, is very much related to a way of life, a personal commitment of lifestyle, not just an academic theory. A person who lives *t'sedeka* seeks to live justly and to bring justice eventually to all.[8]

Another key word is *t'shuvah*, which means 'a halt' so that things can turn around. It contains the notion of conversion and repentance. A person who stops drinking alcohol because of problems, practises *t'shuvah*. Bianchi argues that the modern law must allow the opportunity for *t'shuvah*, a turnaround, to be accomplished.[9]

Hesed is an important word and reflects the love that contains justice as its motivating force. *Mishpat* reflects the social expression of God's justice in the relationship of God with the people, and the people with one another.

Wayne Northey gives us some hints on how to interpret what, at first sight, appear to be retributive passages in scripture:

- Judaic law is much broader and deeper than Western state law. It is primarily theological and conveys, as indicated, all the dimensions of the relationship between God and humanity. It was not simply narrowly concerned with legal or criminal data.

- The law codes were really in fact only quasi-legal. The primary purpose of the law was to create a people of God who would adhere to God's will. The concern was thus much more religious than criminal, or even civil.

- Some of the language seen to be most legally orientated was actually homiletical, exhorting God's people to holiness. The writing was often as if the Israelites were living according to God's law. (cf Exodus 23/22-4).

- Some of the references to prohibitions and punishments are more descriptive than prescriptive – as much describing an actual event as a warning, indicating it should or should not happen again. (cf Leviticus 20/27, Numbers 15/36).

- It is probable that a ritualistic form of expiation or atonement in the temple, rather than an applied punishment, accompanied the redress of crimes or sins in the bulk of cases. (cf Numbers 16, Leviticus 4, Leviticus 6/1-7). Otherwise, compensation was the norm, not so much seen as a punitive measure but as a means of making peace come to all concerned.[10]

As scripture scholar Virginia Mackey concludes, in their scripture and tradition, Jews have urged caution in judgment, have shown reluctance to punish, and have exhibited the desire to make atonement, restitution or reconciliation after conflicts. This is their interpretation of 'making right', 'making peace', or 'achieving *shalom*'. The predominant theology is one of restoration.

Perry Yoder, a distinguished biblical studies professor, says that while retributive justice is found in the First Testament, it is often in the context of *shalom* justice, whereby the motive for it being meted out is setting things right.[12]

Shalom and Covenant

The two most central concepts of biblical law and justice relate to *shalom* and covenant. Howard Zehr points out that *shalom* is not just a peripheral theme of scripture but a basic core belief from which God's vision and plan for creation and the development of the human family flow. Hence notions of salvation, atonement, forgiveness and justice have their roots in *shalom*.[13]

In English *shalom* is usually translated to mean peace, but that is a very inadequate translation. Perry Yoder describes three basic dimensions to its meaning. They are physical wellbeing, including adequate food, clothing, shelter and wealth; a right relationship between and among people; and the acquisition of virtue, especially honesty and moral integrity. The absence of *shalom* means the absence of one or other of these features.[14]

There is a flow-on of this concept in the New Testament where Christ's life and teachings and eventually his death and resurrection transform relationships between and among people, thus inaugurating the Reign of God, the New Creation, wherein *shalom* – justice, peace, righteousness – are lived by believers.

The other major concept that has a direct relationship with law and justice is that of covenant. A covenant is a binding agreement between parties. There were several in the scriptures, starting with God and creation in Genesis. Then there was the one with Abraham, Sarah and the newly created People of God, followed by the one with God and Moses representing the people on Mount Sinai when the Ten Commandments were given.

The culminating covenant came with Jesus and the whole of humanity at the Last Supper. This was enacted through the suffering and death of Jesus on the cross at Calvary and through the resurrection, and subsequently ritualised at the celebration of the Eucharist or Mass. This new covenant opened up for humanity a new way of viewing things, of relating, of recognising the dignity of each person within the context of their community.

Tragically over the centuries the Church has often been a far from benign influence on the development of just social structures, including the criminal justice system prevalent in the West. However, this does not exclude its potential to yet fulfil something of the vision of which the ancient prophets dreamed and for which Jesus died.

In his seminal book on restorative justice, *Changing Lenses,* Howard Zehr says that biblical justice seeks to make things right, and this often means liberation for the unequal. Thus biblical justice shows a clear partiality towards those who are oppressed and impoverished. It is clearly on the side of the poor, recognising their needs and disadvantages. Biblical justice is open-eyed, with hands outstretched to those in need.

He goes on to say that since biblical justice seeks to make things better, justice is not designed to maintain the status quo. Indeed, its intent is to shake up the status quo, to improve, to move towards *shalom*. The move towards *shalom* is not necessarily good news for everyone. In fact it is downright bad news for the oppressor. It also stands in contrast to that justice which, by working to maintain order, works in fact to maintain the present order, the status quo, even when it is unjust.

The test of justice in the biblical view is not whether the right rules are applied in the right way. Justice is tested by the outcome. The tree is tested by its fruit. It is the substance, not the procedure, that defines justice. And how should things come out? The litmus test is how the poor and oppressed are affected.[15]

In biblical times such justice was enacted on an everyday basis in Jewish settlements. Citizens went to the city gates to seek justice from the judges or elders who presided there for this purpose. The whole focus for this 'court' setting was to find a solution for the aggrieved person. As Karl Barth points out, the judge was not primarily the one who rewarded some (distributive justice). He was the one who created order and restored what had been destroyed.

Restoration, then, was the keynote, not retribution. The words in Hebrew for 'paying back' and 'recompense', *shillum* and *shillem,* have the same root words as *shalom*. Restoring *shalom* was what such courts were all about. Helping people re-establish their covenant with God and one another was at the heart of this justice. When punishment was meted out, and on occasion this included execution, it was always seen as a necessary element to the restoration of the covenant and the re-establishment of *shalom.*

As Zehr says, biblical law was intended as a means, not an end in itself. The best law was unwritten law, and it was the spirit, not the letter, of the law that mattered. This was the original focus of the Torah, but in time it became rigidified. It was this legalism, this rigidity, that Christ so objected to. This perspective also helps to explain why so often the spirit rather than the letter of the law seemed to be carried out in the First Testament. As Christ points out in his comments about the Sabbath, law was made for people, not people for the law. The intent was that 'wise indications' be internalised, that the thrust of the law be followed.[16]

The New Testament and Justice

In the New Testament Jesus clearly states that justice should be based on principles of forgiveness and reconciliation; that retaliation plays no part. He forgave the Genasene maniac, the prostitute, the adulteress, the tax gatherer who was an extortionist, the robber. He charged us both to place distinctions between wrongdoers and the virtuous, but to see ourselves as all in the same camp – brothers and sisters with varying strengths and weaknesses. He rejected any notion of just desserts in the vineyard workers parable (Matthew 20/1-16), and in the story of the prodigal son and loving parent (Luke 15/11-32).

In the story of the rich man and Lazarus (Luke 16/19-31), Jesus explicitly teaches that the poor man has rights and the rich man is obliged out of a sense of justice, not charity, to share what he has from his table. Here Luke draws on Leviticus 25/35, which spells out the obligations of the rich to the poor. The rich man fails to recognise that though he may well have come by his wealth by perfectly legal means, in justice he still owes part of his wealth to Lazarus, who has nothing. He fails and is condemned.

Here Jesus explicitly expounds the nature of justice in terms of sharing with the needy, the poor, the vulnerable. Lazarus and the rich man can only ever meet and be reconciled as brothers through the sharing of the riches. Reconciliation, then, is at the heart of the New Testament understanding of justice. Or, as biblical scholar Ronald Craygrill says, reconciliation among humans is the identifying mark of God's new creation.[17]

Swiss theologian Siegfried Meurer has an interesting reflection on that other very important parable on justice, the vineyard owner and the day labourers, in Matthew 20. In this parable not only are those who wish to question God's right to give to all equally sent away, but so are those who understand justice and goodness to stand in contradiction. Justice must serve life and its sustenance.[18]

Meurer further states that the one who punishes must grant the one punished the possibility of making amends. He concludes that punishment seen as retaliation, whether by the individual or by society, is rejected, for it (retaliation) alone is the reserve of God. Likewise, the state is not allowed to exercise retaliation. He also speaks of the contrast between the Jewish and subsequent Christian understandings of justice, and that of the Roman Empire. The former is restorative emphasising reconciliation with the neighbour, the latter retributive, emphasising the maintenance of order at all cost through the maintenance of law.

Imprisonment in the New Testament

Imprisonment is condemned by New Testament teachings where it represents a power of death that is separate from and opposed to God. Death is also present in other forms, including illness, hunger, injustice and opulence. The proclamation of liberty to captives does not relate simply to a notion of spiritual freedom. Such an interpretation helps make sense of the miraculous nature of the deliverance of the apostles from prison in two instances, Acts 5 and 12. As Griffith says, the releases are an assertion of divine authority over the state and over the fallen principalities and powers. Deliverance is also life-affirming in that it is a renunciation of that death with which imprisonment is biblically identified.[19]

In a reference to the Matthew 25 injunction that Christians should visit the imprisoned, Griffith says that the word used, *episkeptomai*, does not merely mean to visit in our modern sense but to spend time with people and establish relationships and personal contact. The same verb is used to refer to the divine activity of caring for, redeeming and freeing. As such it is a prelude to the reintegration of the prisoner into the community as a full member, restoring that person with a place and full rights.[20]

Sanctuary

A final word on justice at the time of Jesus concerns the notion of sanctuary. It is a further illustration that Jewish law valued life over property, and valued people over punishment. Several mentions are made in the ancient scriptures to cities of refuge (Deuteronomy 4/41-3, 19/1-3, Numbers 35/6-34). Daniel Vanness, in his book *Crime and Its Victims,* says that both Israel and its neighbours recognised the right of a person needing protection from revenge to go to the altar in the temple, where the person was to be kept from harm until the matter could be decided through formal judicial process (Exodus 21/12-14). But the altar might be far away, and the wrongly accused person might be caught before reaching the protection of the sanctuary. So the law provided for six cities of refuge, which were to be centrally located and reached by well-built roads, so that someone suspected of murder could get to protection easily.

People were more important than punishment and, as a result, procedural safeguards were built into the law so that the rights of the offender could be protected while the case was being considered by the judicial authorities.[21]

Sanctuary is a tradition that is not only scriptural but has a civic tradition with a rich and moving history. The concept of sanctuary was so compelling that it was recognised in Roman law, medieval common law and English common law. In the 1600s every church in England could be a sanctuary. During the 17th century the whole of the North American continent was seen as a sanctuary from the political and religious persecutions in Europe.

Two of the most heroic periods of the tradition occurred during the 1850s in the United States and during World War II in Europe. After the passage of the Fugitive Slave Act (1850), which made it illegal to harbour or assist a slave in gaining freedom, some northern churches became stations on the underground railroad in defiance of federal law. More recently many convents, churches and monasteries hid Jews fleeing the Nazis during World War II in defiance of law prohibiting such practices.[22]

Sanctuary has also been used extensively by political and religious refugees who break immigration laws to enter a country. Most recently, sanctuary has been provided by hundreds of church groups of all denominations in the United States in their efforts to help Central American refugees escape torture and death at home. The refugees, mainly from El Salvador and Guatemala, have fled the 'death squads' and the military and police apparatus (mainly trained in the US) that have sought to suppress any social change destined to free the people from poverty, malnutrition, illiteracy and hopelessness.[23]

At the US borders they have been met by tough immigration policies and either detained in refugee camps or sent immediately back to their native countries. For thousands, this has proved to be a death sentence. From the early 1980s many parish churches in the US opened their doors to these fleeing refugees by providing personnel and transport to bypass the border posts and enter the US illegally. More than 70,000 US citizens have actively participated in breaking US immigration law in order to provide sanctuary.[24]

Such law-breaking forms part of the morality of those who seek to provide true justice from a biblical perspective. Like Jesus dealing with accusations of breaking the Sabbath, they simply argue that law is there to serve the wellbeing of the community, and not the rich and powerful elite who benefit from and wish to maintain the status quo in Central America.

Like the Ploughshares activists in the nuclear arms context, they argue that justice and freedom as understood in the sacred scriptures cannot be hindered or contravened by legislation. In a hierarchy of law, those that preserve life are the most important, and immigration laws and laws of property are those that become secondary. They illustrate this by arguing that people are morally allowed to smash their way into burning houses to rescue children even though they damage property on entering, which is against the law.

They pose the question, who would not have attempted to smash open the doors of railway wagons carrying Jews to concentration camps and death because the law says that property damage is illegal? For such people, the law only has true validity when it leads to true justice.

Sanctuaries have been used down through the ages primarily by both those who have committed crimes, including serious crimes, and by refugees escaping oppression. The sanctuary remains inviolable while they negotiate an agreement. Because they offer safety, hope and healing from terror, punishment and fear, sanctuaries are symbols of restorative justice.

Conclusion

Unlike our modern Western system, which looks to the past, biblical justice always looked to the future. It always held up before the people a view of what might be if they remained true to the covenant and sought *shalom*. As Zehr says, biblical justice was an active progressive force seeking to transform the present order into one that was more just. In so doing, it sought in particular to protect the weak, the vulnerable and the poor.

It contained an overall thrust and many constitutive elements that would be of immense benefit to any modern society. Any society could learn from a re-examination of its history, philosophy and practice.[25]

Footnotes

1. Exodus 21/23-25; Leviticus 24/19-20; Deuteronomy 19/21.
2. Herman Bianchi, *New Perspectives on Crime and Justice*, MCC Office of Criminal Justice, Elkhart, Indiana, 1984, p3
3. Lee Griffith, *Alternatives to Calling the Police: Some Biblical and Historical Perspectives*, paper presented at the Christian as Victim Conference, 1982, Kansas City, Missouri. p3
4. Matthew 5/38-42
5. Griffith, op cit, pp3-4
6. Bianchi, op cit, p6
7. Kevin O'Reilly, *Towards a Christian View*, Prison Chaplains' Association, New Zealand, 1982, p3
8. Bianchi, op cit, p3
9. Ibid, p4
10. Wayne Northey, *Justice in Peacemaking: A Biblical Theology of Peacemaking in Response to Criminal Conflict*, MCC US Office of Criminal Justice, Ontario, May 1992, p16
11. Virginia Mackay, *Punishment in the Scripture and the Tradition of Judaism, Christianity and Islam*, National Inter-Religious Taskforce on Criminal Justice, New York, 1982, p2.
12. Perry Yoder, *Shalom: the Bible's Word for Salvation, Justice and Peace*, Faith and Life Press, Newton, Kansas, 1987, p130
13. Howard Zehr, *Changing Lenses*, Herald Press, Scottdale, Pennsylvania, 1990, p133
14. Yoder, op cit, p130
15. Zehr, op cit, pp139-40
16. Ibid, p144
17. Ronald S. Craybrill, *Repairing the Breach: Ministering in Community Conflict*, Herald Press, Scottdale, Pennsylvania, 1981, p12
18. Siegfried Meurer, *Das Recht im Dienst der Versonnung und des Riedens*, Theologischer Verlag, Zurich, 1972
19. Griffith, op cit, p5
20. Ibid, p5
21. Daniel Vanness, *Crime and Its Victims*, Inter-Varsity Press, Leicester, 1986, pp116-17
22. Renny Golden and Michael McConnell, *Sanctuary – the New Underground Railway*, Orbis Books, Maryknoll, NY, 1986, p15
23. Ibid, p2
24. Ibid, p3
25. Zehr, op cit, p146

CHAPTER TWELVE

A Future Paradigm:
Restorative Justice in Aotearoa?

There is a dingy, run-down housing estate in Walstall in England where community organisations are working with the West Midlands Police in setting up a motor project. Young people in the area are given old cars to repair and when they are fixed the youngsters can race them against each other. The whole estate is involved and it costs practically nothing.

It costs $NZ50,000 a year to keep a person in prison. Spending some of that money on projects such as the motor project protects cars and people. It gives the young people some direction and fulfilment, and most no longer end up in prison.[1]

There is a tremendous amount of emotional baggage to any discussions on issues of law and order, crime, prisons, harsher penalties, habilitation centres, safer communities. Many of us have been victims of crime. The law, the police, the government often seem to be impotent in dealing with rising amounts of criminal behaviour in the community. Fear begets more fear.

Many claim that the law is unjust anyway. Others claim that imprisonment makes people worse rather than better. All the various policies tried over the years within the retributive penal system have failed dismally. The straight, hard-labour, bread-and-water routine so popular in the early part of this century brutalised inmates, turning many into incorrigible recidivists. The medical model of corrections whereby everything was seen in terms of therapeutic needs also failed.

The unit-management style currently in vogue will ultimately be seen as a failure too. Programmes are useful in prisons, but the negative framework of punishment in which they are conducted nearly always negates the possibility of substantial positive change. Just as you cannot cure an alcoholic in a brewery, so you cannot reform inmates in a prison.

You cannot punish and reconcile at the same time. Contradictory objectives can only lead to stalemate or total paralysis. This is not a problem of opinion or ideology. It is simply a question of logic.

The case-management system, which the Justice Department applied as its major response to the 1989 Prison Systems Review (Roper Report), seeks to reconcile the contradictory objectives of reform within a punishing environment. Justice Roper said it would not work and he was right. While such an approach does have some positive effects within the prison system, it does not succeed in its aim of changing the basic orientation of inmates. Case management has simply become a better system of control of inmates. It has also allowed the Justice Department to continue to expand its empire and its burgeoning budget, and maintain its power base.

Restorative Justice

Under a philosophy of restorative justice, crime is no longer defined as an attack on the state but rather an offence by one person against another. It is based on a recognition of the humanity of both offender and victim. The goal of the restorative process is to heal the wounds of every person affected by the offence, including the victim and the offender. Options are explored that focus on repairing the damage.

The three key players in the restorative justice equation are the offender, the victim and the community. Obviously, a willingness to co-operate is central to the concept. To be involved in any useful way, the offender must acknowledge responsibility for the crime committed and express honest regret. The full implications of the offence need to be spelt out and confronted. The offender needs also to face the causes of the offending and, where possible, make restitution. Concrete evidence of more appropriate behaviour in the future is also required.

Victims need to examine their feelings and take full advantage of any support network that will facilitate healing. Victims are helped to see that their own victimisation is only intensified by feelings of retributive action against the offender. Where appropriate they become involved in the process of restorative justice with the offender and the community.

The community's role is to create the conditions most favourable to the restoration of both offender and victim. It aids the healing process by providing mediators, judges, supervisors and other appropriately appointed people.

Sometimes in a controlled mediated process the offenders meet the victims and have to face up to what they have done. They hear of the victims' anger and anxiety, and the victims hear the offenders' explanation. There may be mitigating circumstances; there may not. The offender may apologise, may express a genuine wish to change. Provided there is co-operation, the parties reach agreement about repairing the damage.

The important thing is that no-one is shut out of the process. It would be silly to claim that all the damage can be repaired immediately – sometimes it never can be. Certainly in murder and rape cases it can't. But at least those involved get the chance to put a human face on the crime and begin the process of healing. They become empowered again. The offenders get to take some responsibility for their criminal behaviour.

The idea of including compensation, reconciliation, healing and forgiveness into criminal law is more than merely corrective. Such elements reflect a whole fresh way of approaching criminal offending in the community. They present a vision of improving life right throughout the community, and of making justice more effective and fair.

Martin Wright, the policy development officer for Victim Support in London, outlines a possible process of restorative justice this way:

- Restorative justice would have a single primary aim: to restore (or improve) the condition of the victim, where there are individual victims, as far as possible. This would be done by the community through Victim Support; by the offender through reparation; and by the state through criminal injuries compensation for crimes of violence. Ideally there would also be a safety-net compensation scheme for the most disadvantaged victims of the crimes against property.

- Where offenders were known, the sanction would take the form of reparation to the victim or the community.

- Another way in which an offender could make reparation, in some cases, would be by accepting a rehabilitative programme to help him or her avoid future offending (eg a drug or violence programme). Hence there would be a corresponding obligation on the community to ensure that an adequate range of programmes was available.

- Victims would have the right to an opportunity to meet their offenders for mediation if both wished it. This would be dependent on the needs and wishes of the victim and not limited by the seriousness of the offence. It would take place when the victim was ready for it, rather than at a time linked to any one stage of the criminal justice process. It would be especially appropriate when the crime arose from a dispute.

- When an offence was serious enough to cause fear or danger among members of the public, any reparation agreed between the victim and the offender could be supplemented by the court. The measures imposed by the court, however, would be reparative, not punitive, in intent.

- Offenders would be offered the opportunity to make voluntary reparation, but ultimately they would be held accountable by being required to do so. This compulsion would not apply of course to mediation. In those cases in which crime arose from a dispute, both parties would be given the opportunity to settle it through mediation.

• For victims whose offenders were not caught, and offenders whose victims did not wish to meet them, victim-offender groups could be arranged.

• Deprivation of liberty would be imposed only for the protection of the public. It would take two forms: restrictions on activities where necessary for the protection of the public; and custody, imposed only when there was no other way of protecting the public against a major risk of further grave harm.[2]

A restorative paradigm has a number of advantages over traditional criminal justice. Not only would there be a single primary aim instead of the current multiplicity of aims, but also:

1. The response to crime would build on offenders' abilities and good qualities, increase their accountability and, potentially, their understanding, and allow them to earn re-acceptance in the community. It could be proportionate to the offence, provided that it was within the offenders' capacity.

2. Crime prevention policy would be integrated with social policies rather than being a by-product of the response to individual crimes. Those who administer justice could therefore deal with victims and offenders individually, without looking over their shoulders at the supposed deterrent effect on other people.

3. There would be recognition that people's behaviour was influenced by factors other than fear, such as providing incentives, building self-esteem and setting an example. Insofar as people were influenced by the system, they would have the opportunity to respond to its fairness rather than react against its harshness.

4. The response of the state would be ethically acceptable, that is, it would be in line with what is required of its citizens.

5. Victims would be given the opportunity to be directly involved in the process but would not be burdened with responsibility for a decision involving punishment.

6. Offenders would be involved actively, rather than being the passive objects of punishment.

7. The community's involvement would also be required. Where the sense of community was weak, reparative measures would help to strengthen it, for example, by bringing together groups of trained volunteer mediators.[3]

Restorative justice involves a shift from state power to community power. It should be remembered that it is only in recent centuries that the state has come to play such a prominent role in citizens' lives. Prior to that the community retained most power within its local confines.

Ranjini Rebera, a Sri Lankan-born Christian feminist, identifies three images of power: *power over, power to* and *power with. Power over* reflects the typical authoritarian model of the traditional court: the judge in an all-powerful position, everyone else in varying positions determined by relationship to that position. *Power to* can be seen as a source of energy or the ability to create.

Power with reflects the new relationship found with restorative justice. Here members of families work collectively to create a momentum that leads to positive change and growth for them all. This type of power transforms and is available even to the most vulnerable members of the family. No longer are people purely recipients of authoritative directives from on high. Within the restorative structures they become responsible for what will happen or not happen.[4]

Advantages of Restorative Justice
The restorative process offers tremendous advantages over the retributive system. Four stand out:

1. It is indigenous
Maori traditionally operate a system of justice based on the overall good of the community and the desire to restore its wellbeing. A restorative model of justice could be a bridge to partially meeting Maori demands from some quarters for a separate system of criminal justice. Such a process would not fulfil the guarantee of te tino rangatiratanga (absolute authority) contained in article 2 of the Treaty of Waitangi. Nor would it provide the protection of te ritenga Maori guaranteed in article 4, which is part of the oral tradition of the treaty. This tradition allows for the protection of religious freedom and customary law and formed part of the discussion held before the treaty was signed. The power to make law and exercise authority through Maori legal institutions would still not rest with Maori.

But if the current retributive system could adopt the philosophy and praxis of restorative justice, then there would be no essential difference between the philosophy and aims of the system operating and those of traditional Maori justice, be the setting in a courtroom, a marae, or a Pacific Island church hall. Different systems, different procedures and different styles would reflect different cultures. But there would be one philosophy, one aim, one praxis.

2. It places victims at the centre of the justice equation
Under the current retributive system victims are shoved either right outside or stuck on the periphery. How much of the punitive wave of anger that sweeps the country after a particularly nasty crime flows from the unresolved anger, grief, hurt and pain of the victims of crime? We all initially feel like stringing up a thief who has taken our car or burgled our home. But our emotions settle with time and we all know that such a lashing-out would probably do as much damage as the original crime and would not solve anything.

The experience of our youth justice system offers us some positive insights. Given the opportunity, it is amazing how contrite and shamed so many young people become after meeting their victims at a family group conference called under the Children, Young Persons and Their Families Act. It is also noticeable how forgiving, gracious and helpful so many of the victims are towards the offenders once they have been able to put a human face and history on the crime.

Howard Zehr writes of the needs of victims to speak their feelings, to receive restitution, to experience justice. They need answers to questions that plague them such as who was at fault; so often victims blame themselves. But above all else, victims need the experience of forgiveness.

I am not suggesting that forgiveness comes easily, but it is a process of letting go. Victims need to be able to let go of the crime experience so that while it will always – must always – be part of them, it will no longer dominate their lives. Without that, closure is difficult and the wound may fester for years.[5]

In the current retributive system victims so often find themselves mere footnotes in the process of justice. The offender has taken power from them and the criminal law system also denies them power. Re-empowering victims enables them to be healed.

Many years of prison ministry have shown me how little remorse there is among inmates simply because they never have to meet their victims and see the devastation they have caused. This hardening of the arteries of emotion and repression of shame and grief are the principal causes of recidivism and in so many committing even greater crimes upon release. Prison guarantees re-offending.

3. *It offers healing to all involved*

In that amazing 1993 Christmas-week incident in Mangere, played out before the television eyes of the country and referred to in the Introduction, we saw ample evidence of the power that healing and forgiveness can play in our daily lives. Most of us have not grown to that level of spiritual wisdom and practice. The grieving Tongan and Samoan communities simply embraced the young driver responsible for the death of the two children and forgave him. His deep shame, his fear, his sorrow, his alienation from the community was resolved.

Of course it did not bring the two little boys back to life, but it gave the watching nation the best Christmas gift we have had for a generation – a gift of loving, forgiveness, reconciliation, a model to emulate. These surely are among the finest qualities known to the human family and can proudly sit alongside others such as courage, honesty, integrity and wisdom.

The dictionary defines forgiveness as a process of ceasing to feel resentment against another. It would appear to include the idea of giving up one's natural impulse to strike back and exact revenge. It is often a very difficult thing to accomplish, particularly in a culture that is staunch and macho in its philosophy. 'Don't get mad, get even' is symptomatic of the philosophy of our modern consumer culture. It reflects the philosophy of revenge.

For victims of crime, forgiveness is letting go of the power that the offence and the offender have over them, while not condoning or excusing that person. It means no longer letting the offence and the offender dominate. Without this experience of forgiveness, without this closure, the wound festers and takes over our lives. It, and the offender, are in control. Real forgiveness allows one to move from victim to survivor.[6]

Offenders are not only punished by the criminal justice system, but severely damaged as well. They don't have to face up to their offending, so they don't grow in responsibility. Offenders are not really held accountable, despite rhetoric to the contrary. Judges often talk about accountability, but what they usually mean is that when you do something wrong, you must take your punishment. Genuine accountability means, first, that when you offend, you need to understand and take responsibility for what you did. Offenders need to be encouraged to understand the real human consequences of their actions.

But accountability has a second component as well: offenders need to be encouraged to take responsibility for making things right, for righting the wrong.[7]

Just as victims need an experience of forgiveness, so do offenders. How else can they put the past behind them and positively confront the future? The retributive criminal philosophy provides little encouragement and virtually no room for an offender to confess, repent, change direction, turn life around, admit responsibility and make things right. The justice system simply encourages anger, rationalisation, denial of guilt and responsibility, feelings of powerlessness and dehumanisation. As with victims, the wounds just fester and grow.[8]

It is interesting to note that in Japan, which has a very low imprisonment rate of 37 per 100,000 (the US has 520 per 100,000), forgiveness is a central part of the criminal justice philosophy. Letters of apology from the offenders to their victims are frequently followed by letters from the victim to the police asking that criminal proceedings be dismissed.[9]

Forgiveness is not something that the victim does for the benefit of the offender. It is the process of the victim letting go of the rage and pain of the injustice so that he or she can resume living freed from the power of the criminal violation. We encounter injustice daily in our homes, our places of work and in the affairs of nations. We can ill afford to respond to the grievances, large or small, in ways that are likely to escalate conflict and perpetuate cycles of violence. In many situations it is precisely the quest for justice as retribution that prevents many grievances from ever being channelled into forums that can bring resolution and redress. Limiting justice to retribution turns interpersonal disputes into tit-for-tat feuds, and border skirmishes into fully fledged wars.[10]

4. It places responsibility for crime in the hands of those who commit it

Restorative justice brings a dimension of community responsibility into being. It recognises that we all form part of the one human family and that we have responsibilities towards one another. To focus always on the individual as if we always exist outside a grouping at work, at home, in the community, in a sports club – wherever – is to focus too narrowly. It is one of the great weaknesses of the Western judicial system.

Sheeting home responsibility for criminal behaviour to the individual in the context of family and friends usually brings massive shame and regret to offenders. How often have I sat in jail and talked to burglars who had done 20, or 30, or 80 burglaries, and still have no comprehension of the damage done in peoples' lives? To them it is simply property stolen to feed their families, their drug habits, or their greed. It is the same with most other offenders. Only a tiny percentage ever face the reality of what they have done.

Their general approach towards a system that treats them like schoolchildren is that once their punishment is done, there is no more need to worry. 'I've done my time' becomes their catchcry. They have had their 'just desserts', says the state. They have paid their debt to society. There is clearly no room for either victims or positive change in such a scenario.

A Case History

Judge Fred McElrea has already applied the principles of restorative justice in the District Court in Auckland. Even without new legislation, there already exists enough flexibility in the court processes to enable this to happen.

In June 1994 a 21-year-old man called Barry appeared on charges of robbery, assault and theft involving $700. He had been remanded in custody to Mt Eden Prison by another judge. The offences involved two incidents that occurred some weeks apart. In the first a handbag had been snatched from an elderly woman who was also assaulted. The second involved the theft of money from a Chinese takeaway. Judge McElrea decided it was an appropriate case to be dealt with by way of a restorative process.

The accused was granted bail. Then the offender, the takeaway victims, a friend of the assaulted woman, the police, and the supporters of both sides and families all came together at a community group conference (CGC). Rev Doug Mansill, a Presbyterian minister, acted as mediator.

All present at the meeting aired their feelings. The victims' families felt Barry had an 'attitude problem' but they felt imprisonment was not going to help. They wanted him to return the money and repair the damaged till. The assaulted woman's friend spoke of the fear such a frail woman would have when a big man robbed her. She invited Barry to stand alongside her as she spoke, just to make the size difference apparent to him. She reminded him he should learn to say 'no' when trouble was brewing, and to take personal responsibility for his behaviour.

Barry's father and mother then spoke of their family's sorrow at their son's behaviour and expressed deep regret to the victims. The arresting police officer also spoke and noted that Barry had shown remorse after he had been charged.

Finally Barry spoke. He apologised for his behaviour and said he had learnt a lot of positive things from the experience. These especially related to how much his family cared for him. He asked those present not to hold his family responsible as it was he who had committed the offences.

Members of the family then met alone to make recommendations regarding an appropriate response for Barry. They were later joined by the victims, the police and the mediator. Final recommendations were agreed to and prepared for the court.

These were that Barry apologise in writing to all the victims and pay the $700 reparation required by the takeaway owners. Imprisonment was not recommended as the group felt he had learned a valuable lesson through being in custody while on remand. However, it was agreed a sentence of periodic detention or community service should be imposed. Barry also agreed to re-establish contacts with his church and spend more fruitful time with his family. A non-association order was suggested with regard to his co-offender, and Barry sought a temporary curfew between 7pm and 7am to help him become more self-disciplined. He was to seek counselling through the Justice Department, do some more educational courses, and be placed under Community Corrections supervision for nine months.

Barry returned to the court with this series of recommendations. In general the court accepted the proposals, imposing a six-month periodic detention sentence on the robbery charge, and supervision with a 12-month suspended jail sentence on the theft charge. To court veterans it appeared to be a fairly hefty sentence given the circumstances, although another judge could have simply sentenced him to imprisonment. But the comprehensive programme Barry has undertaken, coupled with his genuine desire to stay clear of future trouble, mean that a negative situation has been turned around and a young man's future given a positive direction again.

The victims were very satisfied with the result. The elderly assault victim, who was not present at the CGC, later had a 90-minute talk with Barry and the mediator, which left her feeling satisfied.

It seems important that when rare aggravating circumstances exist the courts should retain the power to reject the recommendation of a CGC and impose a sentence itself. It is a power that should be used sparingly, and is the current practice for youth justice. It should be noted that in 81 percent of the cases in the Maxwell/Morris survey into the results of the Children, Young Persons and Their Families Act, family group conference plans were accepted by the courts. Judge McElrea estimates that in the Auckland region, the largest in New Zealand, this figure was closer to 100 percent acceptance.

He also believes that victims should have some say in the outcome of a judicial process provided they have engaged properly in the process of adjudication. He notes that the idea of negotiated justice rather than imposed justice already has ready parallels in the 1990s. Commercial mediation, arbitration, the police diversion scheme, negotiated settlements to Treaty of Waitangi disputes and the whole move towards proportional representation in Parliament reflect the movement towards negotiated rather than imposed settlements.[11]

The Victim-Offender Reconciliation Programme

The best-known practical programme applying a partial restorative philosophy is the Victim-Offender Reconciliation Programme (VORP), now used in over 130 centres in the US and Canada. Ideally, it is a process that needs to be based in an independent organisation outside the criminal justice system but able to work in co-operation with the police, courts and probation.

The process involves a mediated face-to-face encounter between victim and offender. The offender needs to have admitted the charges. In these meetings, the emphasis is upon three elements: facts, feelings and agreements. The meeting is facilitated and chaired by a trained mediator, who is preferably a community volunteer.

Once agreement is reached, a written contract is signed. Often this takes the form of financial restitution, but that is not the only possibility. Offenders may agree to work for victims. Sometimes victims ask rather that offenders work for the community, and a community service agreement may be signed.

These encounters provide the important elements in meeting the needs of both victim and offender. An opportunity to tell their story, get information, recover losses, be accountable, experience reconciliation, and feel that justice has been done. While only about half of all referrals end in meetings, nearly all meetings end in agreements. Most of these agreements (as high as 90 percent in most programmes) are fulfilled. Victim satisfaction is high.[12]

One of the first assessments of VORP made by the Brooklyn Dispute Resolution Centre in the late 1970s found that three-quarters of the victims found the outcome to be fair and satisfactory, while slightly more than half of victims who had been through a traditional court experience felt as satisfied. It was the same in 1985 in Brooklyn, New York, where 83 percent of offenders and 59 percent of victims were satisfied with the VORP experience, and another 30 percent of victims were 'somewhat satisfied'.

The reasons underlying these responses are equally alike. Victims express satisfaction for the opportunity to confront the offender to obtain better understanding of the crime and the offender's circumstances; the opportunity to receive compensation for the loss or injury; the expression of remorse by offenders; and the concern and caring responses of the mediators. Surveys of other VORP efforts in the US, Canada and Britain reveal similar levels of victim satisfaction.[13]

In the US, victims and offenders are not required to participate but they usually want to. Meetings take place in 68 percent of the cases. When they take advantage of the reconciliation process, 86 percent of victims and offenders are satisfied with the results.[14]

In Germany, Austria and Finland, in conjunction with the development of a restorative justice philosophy, there has been a substantial re-orientation of judges' sentencing patterns. This is an area that requires careful consideration in any transition towards the adoption of a more restorative philosophy. The experiences of VORP-type programmes in Germany and Finland parallel with extraordinary similarity those in the US.

Victim-offender mediation and an approach to criminal justice that emphasises the restoration of relationships and reintegration of offenders into the community has proven to be successful in every society – from Japan to Switzerland, the US to Finland – in which it has been attempted.[15]

In Germany, in conjunction with VORP programmes, judges introduced a new sentencing philosophy based more on a restorative justice model. During the period 1983-88 the overall imprisonment receival rate decreased by about 3.5 percent a year, while in Western Europe generally it increased by about 3 percent annually. The average daily rate of imprisonment fell by 12.5 percent during that time. From 1984 to 1991 the prison population in Germany fell from 48,500 to 32,500. During this period, crime rates remained virtually static in most areas of offending, including violent crimes. Once again the imprisonment rate was see to bear no correlation to the crime rate.[16]

The British Home Office reviewed all of the victim-offender programmes in Britain. It found that, as in the US, victims express extremely high levels of satisfaction both in terms of the fairness of the process and the opportunity to participate. Through mediated contracts victims received higher levels of compensation than as a result of mandatory orders. Lower rates of recidivism reflected improvement in offender behaviour.

Victims consistently report their appreciation for having the opportunity to tell their stories and to confront offenders with their sense of injury, anger and outrage.

Responses by offenders show more frequent acknowledgment of guilt, deeper appreciation for the consequences of their wrongdoing and a greater sense of remorse. The statistics from carefully monitored evaluations of a variety of programmes evidence the extraordinary success of victim-offender mediation and the validity of its claims of its proponents.[17]

Probably the best model to reflect upon is the process of the Children, Young Persons and Their Families Act, which has been tremendously successful in New Zealand. Since the act came into force in 1989, using a restorative philosophy and the family group conference as its principle mechanism, the number of young offenders appearing before the courts has dropped from 13,000 cases a year to 1800. In the first five years of the act, criminal offending by young people in the 17-20 age group fell by 27 percent. It is obviously a very successful process.

New Zealand's principal Youth Court judge, Michael Brown, says the primary objectives of a criminal justice system must include healing the breach of social harmony and social relationships, putting right the wrong, and making reparation rather than concentrating on punishment. The ability of the victim to have input at the family group conference is, or ought to be, one of the most significant virtues of the youth justice procedures. On the basis of our experience to date, we can expect to be amazed at the generosity of spirit of many victims and (to the surprise of the professionals participating) the absence of retributive demands and vindictiveness. Victims' responses are in direct contrast to the hysterical, media-generated responses to which we are so often exposed.[18]

The New Zealand police are equally enthusiastic. Senior Sergeant Laurie Gabites of Police National Headquarters, Wellington, sees the act as law that has offered the community more benefits than many other pieces of legislation. It has offered benefits for both victims and offenders. It has offered offenders a chance to participate in the decision-making. It has offered help and support for victims and given them a chance to play a part in the justice system that has probably never been equalled anywhere else in the world.

It has also involved families in a way that has seen them making decisions about breaches of the law by way of consensus. He believes the law deserves closer examination as a blueprint for legislation to be applied to adults.[19]

Gabrielle Maxwell, senior researcher with the Commission for Children, studied the act in its first three years of operation.

> We looked at nearly 700 young offenders. We looked at over 200 cases which went to a family group conference and 70 cases that appeared in the Youth Court. I want to celebrate some of the successes we saw at that time. I want to allay some of the myths there are about the problems with the FGCs and I also want to identify some of the weaknesses, bearing in mind that this was 1990 and 1991, just a year after the act got under way and I think we need time to learn

how to operate a new system. In fact in some ways I want to stress how extraordinary these successes are in such a revolutionary endeavour.[20]

Praise for the act comes from Australia too. Criminologist John Braithwaite, of the Australian National University, Canberra, writes that reforms to the New Zealand juvenile justice system since 1989 have had the effect of bringing shame and personal and family accountability for wrongdoing back into the justice process.

He says if the young offender's football coach is a person looked upon with respect, then he could be invited to the FGC. Braithwaite has attended a conference with 30 members of the community in the room. Conservative politicians who say they want to strengthen the family and do something for victims as the forgotten people in the criminal process should support this process, Braithwaite says.[21]

New Zealand's Future: Restorative Justice for Adults

Many people said in years past that the youth justice system was beyond reform. Our history of Social Welfare homes, borstals, detention centres, youth prisons and corrective training was one of failure, yet because they were such a part of an entrenched retributive and punishing philosophy, little could be done to change the situation. It was all a part of our English retributive heritage, and the radical shift needed to really make any substantial difference would never happen. History has shown such sceptics to be wrong.

The question now has to be how do we translate the successful youth restorative philosophy and practice into the adult criminal justice system? How do we create an adult model of restorative justice?

The first area we need to look at is the nature of community. Tony Marshall, a leading British expert on penal philosophy, argues that the concept of community can be expanded to accommodate the fact that our society allows meaningful association based on leisure pursuits, political parties, churches, ethnic groups, trade unions and extended families.[22]

Could the family group conference of youth justice be translated into an adult version? In most instances, I believe it can quite easily. Such a conference would not need to be large, though it could be. For Pakeha, if there were few family or friends to call upon, the conference might entail a gathering of only two or three, including the offender. For Maori and Pacific Islanders, where the bonding of whanau is still usually strong, there should not be a problem.

The group could be called, in the words of Judge McElrea, a community group conference (CGC). He proposes that a co-ordinator would invite to that conference the victim (and supporters, if desired), a police representative, family members if appropriate, and people representing other significant relationships for the offender. Imagination and perseverance would be necessary to assemble a community group. If, despite skilled endeavour, no-one could be found, there may be a place for voluntary associations. For example, a local church group, cultural association or service organisation could step into the gap. An agency offering assistance to address a specific need (illiteracy, alcoholism, budgeting help) might appropriately be included in a CGC.

If an adult system was to follow on the youth justice model it would have diversionary mechanisms, in particular restrictions on the arresting or summonsing of offenders so that a CGC could consider alternatives to prosecution. If agreed by all members of the CGC (including the victim and the police) no prosecution would ensue and the matter would be dealt with as decided by the CGC, that is in the community.

The police would need the power to arrest in some form (as with young people) where it is necessary to prevent further offending or ensure the offender's attendance at court, or prevent interference with evidence. The police might argue for the right to arrest persistent offenders, or those to be charged with serious offences, say purely indictable offences, or perhaps a combination of these two criteria.

McElrea would argue it would be unwise to bypass the CGC process altogether for such offenders. Of course serious cases are still likely to result in a term of imprisonment, either as an agreed outcome of a CGC or because it is thought necessary by the court, but there is nevertheless likely to have been value in the CGC in terms of the restoration of the victim's rights and assistance to the court in sentencing.

> For very serious offences, for example rape, the victim may not be ready to face the offender for some time, even years, after the event. This should not be a reason to avoid a CGC. A representative of the victim would be entitled to act on behalf of the victim, and I believe there should be an obligation on behalf of the offender to meet with the victim at some later point, if and when the victim would find that helpful. Any further step to be taken at that point would be purely voluntary.[23]

It is obvious there are going to be different outcomes in like cases. The Youth Court model applies the same law throughout the land, as indeed would any adult court. It is important for courts to retain their overseeing role, not the least to guard against the possibility of oppressive custom or sexist or racist outcomes. Critical attention needs to be paid to the assumption that our existing system of justice does treat like cases alike. In reality, since uniformity and flexibility are competing elements of justice, equal treatment can be achieved only at the expense of possibly doing injustice in individual cases.

It needs to be noted that while there are now more sentencing guidelines handed down from the Court of Appeal to guide judges, there has been a long tradition of freedom for judges to consider all the facts before them and take independent sentencing options.

To illustrate, in one particular week in May 1994 two men in different towns were given widely different sentences after each appeared for his 24th conviction of driving while disqualified. One was sentenced in the Wellington District Court to six months' jail suspended for 12 months, six months periodic detention, and disqualification from driving for 12 months. In the Whakatane District Court, Judge Ron Gilbert gave the other defendant hope for an entirely fresh start to his life by applying no further penalty and by wiping a previous disqualification and a previous suspended sentence, thus 'giving the man a chance to return to life as a worker and as a father'. As a result the man can apply for a new licence and was encouraged to remain out of trouble from then on.

Conclusion

Some dimensions of restorative justice already have widespread support in New Zealand. In early 1994 a *Listener*/Heylen poll found that in response to the statement 'offenders should meet with their victims and where possible try to put things right', 55 percent agreed or agreed strongly, while a further 20 percent were either neutral or didn't know. Only a quarter disagreed. In response to a further statement that we should 'place more emphasis on probation where offenders may be supervised in the community', 62 percent agreed or agreed strongly, a further 20 percent were either neutral or didn't know, and only 18 percent disagreed.

It would appear that, contrary to radio talkback wisdom, there is a reasonable foundation in the wider community prepared to accept a structural move away from imprisonment towards more positive, restorative, non-custodial options in New Zealand.

We are at a critical juncture in the history of criminal sanction. We doubled our prison population between 1986 and 1994 and, if projections are followed, we are set to add the same number again by 1998. This marked increase has not reduced crime. If anything, it has guaranteed more spectacular future serious offending. It has certainly helped create tougher, more embittered and harder individuals whose crimes upon release will in many instances be more savage, more brutal, more irresponsible.

The argument of this book is that our retributive philosophy is at fault. We have a simple choice. We can continue down our current road and end up with the 6000 prisoners-plus projected by 1998, at a cost to the taxpayer of about $400 million a year. This course of action will also guarantee us a continued rise in crime rates. We will all need to guard our persons and property much more securely. It will also make for a much greater level of fear, division and alienation within the community.

Or we can reappraise our retributive system and all its works and pomp. We can decide collectively that it really is a massive failure in most senses of that word. And we can choose to change. We can choose to start building on the successful model that has applied to youth justice and translate it into an adult process. We can stop building more and more prisons, and start using the vast resources saved to create a new system built not on vengeance and punishment, but on reconciliation, personal responsibility, healing, forgiveness, accountability and, where applicable, sanction.

The whole nation can only benefit from such a change.

Footnotes

1. Vivien Stern, Cantor Lecture, 'Crime, Policy and the Role of Punishment', London, *RAS Journal*, October 1993
2. Martin Wright, paper from *Restorative Justice on Trial*, ed Heinz Messmer and Hans-Uwe Otto, NATO Scientific Series, Kluwer Academic Publishers, London, 1992, pp528-30
3. Ibid, p530
4. *The Tablet* (NZ), 16 January 1994
5. Howard Zehr, *IARCA Journal*, March 1991, pp6-8
6. Howard Zehr, *Changing Lenses*, Herald Press, Scottdale, Pennsylvania, 1990
7. Howard Zehr, op cit
8. Ibid
9. John Haley, paper from *Restorative Justice on Trial*, ed Heinz Messmer and Hans-Uwe Otto, NATO Scientific Series, Kluwer Academic Publishers, London, 1992, p105
10. Dean Peacey, ibid, p557
11. F. W. M. McElrea, 'New Zealand Youth Court: A Model for Development in Other Courts?', paper presented at the National Conference of District Court Judges, Rotorua, New Zealand, 8 April 1994
12. Virginia Mackay, *Restorative Justice: Towards Non-violence*, Presbyterian Criminal Justice Programme,. Louisville, Kentucky, 1990
13. John Haley, *Crime and Justice Network Newsletter,* Mennonite Central Committee, Akron, Pennsylvania, September 1991
14. Daniel W. Vanness, *Crime and Its Victims*, Inter-Varsity Press, Leister 1986
15. John Haley, Mennonite Newsletter
16. Richard Harding, 'Why Do We Send Offenders to Prison and Are We Achieving Our Goals?', paper presented at Prison, the Last Option conference, published by the Anglican, Catholic and Uniting Church of Australia, Perth, 1991
17. John Haley, Mennonite Newsletter
18. M. J. A. Brown, Viewpoint, *Listener*, 25 September 1993
19. L. Gabites, New Zealand Law Conference transcript, 4 March 1993
20. Gabrielle Maxwell, Law Conference transcript
21. John Braithwaite, *The Youth Court in New Zealand A New Model of Justice*, Legal Research Foundation, No 34, 1993
22. Tony Marshall, quoted by Vivienne Morrell, Social Change and Criminal Justice Issues Report, September 1993
23. McElrea, op cit

Glossary

Maori

Aotearoa	traditional name for New Zealand believed given by Maori explorer Kupe, now in general use as an alternative name
aroha	love
hara	crime, offence
hapu	sub-tribe
hui	gathering, meeting
iwi	tribe, people
karakia	prayers
kaumatua	elder
kawanatanga	government
kei te pai	all right, OK, good
kuia	woman elder, old wise woman
mana	personal standing, prestige, influence, power
Maori	name given to the indigenous people of Aotearoa/New Zealand
marae	meeting ground
marama	light, daylight
matuatanga	parenting role
mea tuhonohono	bringing harmony, togetherness
muru	rob, plunder, confiscate
Ngai Tahu	major tribe in the South island
Ngati Kahu	North Island tribe
Ngati Porou	major tribe on the East Coast, North island
Ngati Te Rangi	tribe on the west coast, North Island
Ngati Ranginui	tribe on the west coast, North Island
Nga Puhi	major tribe in Northland
Pakeha	name given by Maori to those of European descent
pakeke	adult, difficult
putao	widow

rangatira	chief, elder
ritenga Maori	Maori custom
rongopai	Gospel
runanga	council of elders
Tainui	major North Island tribe
taha wairua	spiritual matters
tangata	person, people
tangi	funeral, tears, weeping
taniko	embroided border
taonga	treasures
tapu	sacred, forbidden, of the gods
taua muru	raiding party
tikana Maori	Maori customs, rules
tikana o nga hara	criminal code
tino rangatiratanga	sovereignty
tipuna	ancestors
tohunga	expert, specialist, priest
Te Wai Pounamu	South Island
utu	price, revenge
whaikorero	make a speech
whanau	family, including extended family
whakama	shame
whakapapa	geneology, ancestry
whare	house
wharenui	meeting house
wharerunanga	assembly house
whare tangata	sacred personhood

Samoan

'aiga	extended family
ali'i	a high-ranking chief tracing geneology back to the gods
aumaga	a group of untitled men
fa'a Samoa	Samoan lifestyle and traditions
fono	village council of chiefs
'ie toga	fine mat
ifoga	practice of humbling oneself to compensate for an injury
malae	marae, meeting area
mamalu	dignity
mana	influence, power, prestige
Mata'afa	titled chief

matai	a chief
nu'u	district, field
Papalangi	European
tulafale	an orator or a lower-ranking chief with special duties

Aboriginal

janarumi	council of discussion or talk (Jaraldi)
kopara	debt settling, a ritualised response after a birth, death or marriage to restore the accepted spiritual balance
magarada or *manejag*	a gathering involving combat to settle a grievance (Arnhen Land)
moity	family grouping
mulgree	law of Creation
naduni	sickness (Jaraldi)
nathagura	fire ritual (Waranuna)
nildjara	pointing bone (Jaraldi)

Irish

agae fine or	
cenn fine	head of a wide extended family
aigre	a Brehon, an advocate or barrister
breitheamh	a judge
brithem	a Brehon, a judge, an arbitrator
boaire	a big farmer
clann (tuath)	clan, small tribe, petty kingdom
cuirmtig	a regional assembly open to all clansmen
cumal	a unit of value; also a female slave
cumbal senorba	a portion of land set aside for the support widows, orphans and childless elderly couples
Dal	assembly open to heads of scpts and possibly fines
doer	unfree
drui (druid)	priest, prophet, teacher
eiric or eric	a fine for murder or manslaughter
feis	festival
fine	family or extended family
fintiu	land owned by the family
flaithe	a chief of a family or a group of families
flaithe-fine	the male head of the extended family
log n-enech	honour-price, or literally 'the price of his face'
maighin digona	a sanctuary around a house
nemed	a privileged person, sacred, holy

ocaire	a small farmer
oenach	a regular assembly for political, social or commercial transactions. It could also be a fair or community gathering
sept	members of related extended families. Similar to a Maori hapu.
set	a treasure, something of value
slogad	playing host
soer	free
tocomra	a special assembly at which a chief or king might be elected
tuaithe	an area or territory
tuath (pl. tuatha)	common term for a clan, small tribe, petty kingdom

Hebrew

hesed	love/justice
mispat	justice, right relationships
shalom	peace, harmony, wholeness
shillem	recompense
shillum	paying back
t'sedeka	justice, seeking truth
t'shuvah	a halt, a turnabout